BTEC Level 2 First Study Skills Guide in Hospitality

Welcome to your Study Skills Guide! You can make it your own – start by adding your personal and course details below...

Learner's name: _____

BTEC course title: _____

Date started: _____

Mandatory units:

_____

_____

_____

Optional units:

_____

_____

_____

Centre name: _____

Centre address:

_____

_____

_____

Tutor's name: _____

Published by Pearson Education Limited, a company incorporated in England and Wales, having its registered office at Edinburgh Gate, Harlow, Essex, CM20 2JE. Registered company number: 872828

Edexcel is a registered trademark of Edexcel Limited

Text © Pearson Education Limited 2010

First published 2010

13 12
10 9 8 7 6 5 4

British Library Cataloguing in Publication Data
A catalogue record for this book is available from the British Library

ISBN 978 1 84690 924 5

Typeset and edited by DSM Partnership
Cover design by Visual Philosophy, created by eMC Design
Cover photo © PunchStock: BLOOMimage
Printed in Slovakia by Neografia

Acknowledgements

The publisher would like to thank the following for their kind permission to reproduce their photographs:

Alamy Images: ACE STOCK LIMITED 53, MBI 71, 72, Janine Wiedel Photolibrary 15; **Corbis**: 60, Ocean 5; **iStockphoto**: Fontanis 11, Igor Grochev 77/2, Rade Lukovic 12; **Pearson Education Ltd**: Photodisc, Cole Publishing Group, Patricia Brabant 77, Rob Judges 72/2, Steve Shott 24, Ian Wedgewood 34; **TopFoto**: John Powell 20

All other images © Pearson Education

Every effort has been made to trace the copyright holders and we apologise in advance for any unintentional omissions. We would be pleased to insert the appropriate acknowledgement in any subsequent edition of this publication.

Websites

Go to www.pearsonhotlinks.co.uk to gain access to the relevant website links and information on how they can aid your studies. When you access the site, search for either the title BTEC Level 2 First Study Skills Guide in Hospitality or ISBN 9781846909245.

Disclaimer

This material has been published on behalf of Edexcel and offers high-quality support for the delivery of Edexcel qualifications.
This does not mean that the material is essential to achieve any Edexcel qualification, nor does it mean that it is the only suitable material available to support any Edexcel qualification. Edexcel material will not be used verbatim in setting any Edexcel examination or assessment. Any resource lists produced by Edexcel shall include this and other appropriate resources.Copies of official specifications for all Edexcel qualifications may be found on the Edexcel website: www.edexcel.com

Contents

Popular progression pathways

General qualification	Vocationally related qualification	Applied qualification
Undergraduate Degree	BTEC Higher National	Foundation Degree
GCE AS and A level	BTEC National	Advanced Diploma
GCSE	BTEC First	Higher (L2) and Foundation (L1) Diplomas

Your BTEC First course

Early days

Every year many new learners start BTEC Level 2 First courses, enjoy the challenge and successfully achieve their award. Some do this the easy way; others make it harder for themselves.

Everyone will have different feelings when they start their course.

Case study: Thinking positively

Debbie is 14 and very excited about starting a BTEC Level 2 First in Hospitality at school. She hopes it will lead her on a path towards her chosen career, working in hospitality and catering.

Although she is very excited about the opportunities ahead of her she has some questions. She didn't know whether she would have to wear a uniform, what she would look like and exactly what she would be doing on the course.

She decided that it would be useful to visit the course tutor and discuss her queries. The course tutor is able to show her the appropriate uniforms and explains some scenarios where she may have to wear a them. The uniforms are really smart and everyone in the group would wear them.

Visiting and meeting the course tutor is a very positive experience, reminding Debbie that meeting new people is something she really enjoys doing. She realises that wearing the uniforms would give her a sense of being part of the group as everyone would wear them at the same time, and it gives her a realistic context to the training she would receive.

Debbie learns from this situation that if she has questions it is always best to find out the answers rather than worry about not knowing something. Having a positive outlook can help to improve all aspects of life and reduce anxiety when feeling stressed or nervous.

About your course

What do you know already?

If someone asks you about your course, could you give a short, accurate description? If you can, you have a good understanding of what your course is about. This has several benefits.

Four benefits of understanding your course

1. You will be better prepared and organised.
2. You can make links between the course and the world around you.
3. You can check how your personal interests and hobbies relate to the course.
4. You will be alert to information that relates to topics you are studying, whether it's from conversations with family and friends, watching television or at a part-time job.

Read any information you have been given by your centre. Also check the Edexcel website for further details – go to www.edexcel.com.

Interest/hobby	How this relates to my studies

What else do you need to know?

Five facts you should find out about your course

1. The type of BTEC qualification you are studying.

2. How many credits your qualification is worth.

3. The number of mandatory units you will study and what they cover.

4. How many credits the mandatory units are worth.

5. The number of optional units you need to study in total and the options available in your centre.

Case study: Lunch club

Sophie is 15. She has been studying on her BTEC Level 2 First in Hospitality course for a year. She really enjoys the hands-on style the course offers.

'I'm a practical person and learn far more through actually making products than I would from reading about it from a cookery book. Sometimes I make mistakes but because my tutor has lots of knowledge we manage to turn most of them around. It's frustrating when a meal goes a little wrong, but my tutor reassured me that it doesn't matter because learning to turn things around is a really important skill.

'Last year on Wednesdays, with help from our tutor, we ran a lunch club. This involved planning a menu, buying the ingredients, preparing and cooking the food, then serving it to members of staff who are charged to cover costs. It's run like a real restaurant. When I first heard about it it seemed a bit daunting – I'd never had to think about these things before. However, the tutor explained everything to me bit by bit at the times I needed to learn about them.

'My first job at the school lunch club job was to take the money at the till. I was nervous because maths isn't my strongest subject and I thought I might get the change wrong. I was looking forward to speaking to our customers because I'm quite comfortable with that. The lunch club taught me how to be a good host. It's also made me much more confident and recently got a Saturday job waitressing because of it.'

BTEC FACT

BTEC First Certificate = 15 credits

BTEC First Extended Certificate = 30 credits

BTEC First Diploma = 60 credits

Generally, the more credits there are, the longer it takes to study for the qualification.

TRY THIS

Find out which optional units your centre offers. To check the topics covered in each unit go to www.edexcel.com.

TOP TIPS

If you have a choice of optional units in your centre and are struggling to decide, talk through your ideas with your tutor.

Activity: How well do you know your course?

Complete this activity to check that you know the main facts. Compare your answers with a friend. You should have similar answers except where you make personal choices, such as about optional units. Your tutor can help you complete task 9.

1 The correct title of the BTEC award I am studying is:

2 The length of time it will take me to complete my award is:

3 The number of mandatory units I have to study is:

4 The titles of my mandatory units, and their credit values, are:

5 The main topics I will learn in each mandatory unit include:

Mandatory unit	Main topics

6 The number of credits I need to achieve by studying optional units is:

7 The titles of my optional units, and their credit values, are:

8 The main topics I will learn in each optional unit include:

Optional unit	Main topics

9 Other important aspects of my course are:

10 After I have achieved my BTEC First, my options include:

Introduction to the hospitality industry

The hospitality industry is exciting and diverse, and provides many possibilities for employment, travel and progressive career paths. There are many types and styles of hospitality outlets and establishments. These include:

- hotels
- restaurants
- pubs, bars and nightclubs
- contract food service providers (eg corporate hospitality, school canteens, prison catering)
- hospitality services
- membership clubs
- events.

When providing food and drink in the hospitality industry your place of work could range from a fine dining restaurant to a fast food outlet.

People that work within the hospitality industry provide or support the provision of food, drink and accommodation. Their aim is to meet the needs and requirements of the guests. The guests or customers are one of the most important aspects of hospitality. The guests could be from the local area or from anywhere in the UK, or they may be international visitors from all around the world. They might be tourists, business people or family groups. The is a wide variety of people with many different social and cultural backgrounds involved in hospitality, either as staff or guests, and this brings a really exciting aspect to the industry.

Working in hospitality can be very rewarding. Often managers within the hospitality industry have progressed through various job roles in order to get to their current positions. There are opportunities for all employees to progress within hospitality if they are hard working and motivated.

Skills you need for the hospitality industry

There are many skills that are needed in the hospitality industry. This is because the industry is so diverse, and different skills can be needed in the different areas of hospitality.

Social and interpersonal skills

Social and interpersonal skills apply to most aspects of hospitality. If you are a member of staff working front-of-house, then it is important that you are able to talk to customers and guests. Even staff who work behind the scenes must deal with people – both internal customers as well as guest – more often then you may think. In the hospitality industry you will continually deal with people, so your social skills are very important. If working front of house, you are the public face of the business, and much repeat business stems from generating a good working relationship with customers.

Case study: Investigating the hospitality industry

Jason has just started his BTEC Level 2 First in Hospitality. The first unit involves investigating the hospitality industry. Jason is 14 and has little experience of the industry, so this is a good way to start the course.

Initially he starts by researching on the internet the various types of establishment and the different types of operation in the hospitality industry. This includes finding out about the facilities and services that each type of establishment offers. He finds, for example, that hotels offer so many different facilities, like gyms, swimming pools, internet cafes, spa treatments and saunas.

Once Jason has undertaken this initial research, his class has the opportunity to visit some local establishments. Jason finds this really fascinating and it excites him about possibilities for his course. He collects a lot of information when he visits hotels to keep for his coursework.

The careers within hospitality are of particular interest to Jason, and he finds out more about the job roles and responsibilities of the various positions that might suit him.

Jason is also interested in the possibilities of working abroad in the future. This sounds really good as it would give him a chance to travel. There are so many different opportunities for work, finding out more about them is really interesting.

Practical skills

There are a variety of practical skills that used within the hospitality industry. The specific practical skills that you will need will depend on the area you work in and your particular role. You may prefer working front of house or behind the scenes.

The practical skills required to work within a kitchen brigade will involve, for example:

- menu planning
- food preparation techniques
- cooking processes.

Other necessary skills include health and safety awareness, food hygiene and preparation of dishes from a range of commodities. Preparation skills will include knife skills for cutting and chopping food, preparing meals using a range of cooking methods and techniques, and the presentation of final dishes.

Team working skills

Being able to work well in a team is very important when in a kitchen environment. As a member of the kitchen brigade, you will often work in confined areas and may not be able to leave the kitchen during a shift. You will need to be able to communicate quickly and efficiently with the other chefs and with the waiting staff. Various parts of a meal can be produced by different sections in the kitchen, so the timing of the separate parts needs to be perfect in order that the dishes work well.

Numeracy and literacy skills

Aspects of kitchen management, such as calculating costs and menu creation, require good levels of numeracy and literacy. Chefs are often in charge of ordering food and ingredients, and they need to know stock levels and ordering requirements. Chefs are also required in most establishments to calculate gross profits on food sales. These tasks will involve working with figures and percentages.

If you become a chef you will have to know the amounts of ingredients you may need.

Planning and organising skills

When working front of house, you will need skills for the planning and organisation required to run small-scale hospitality events. Tasks include providing food and beverage services, meeting and greeting guests. Planning and running events and functions can often require media and ICT skills to create menus and invitations. Photography and image manipulation can also be useful skills for menu creation, and you may need to photograph food or locations.

Organisational skills are very important for all aspects of working within the hospitality industry and are developed throughout the BTEC hospitality course. If working in a kitchen, you will have to organise your stock, ensuring it is rotated correctly and it has not gone out of date. You will have to organise the ordering, delivery and storage of new stock. If you are in charge of the kitchen, you may have to organise the kitchen staff rotas and the menus for the establishment.

Restaurant managers have to organise seating plans and make sure tables are used to maximise the number of covers for each service. They will also organise the waiting staff and the tables that they each serve.

Physical skills

Having a good sense of balance and spatial awareness is also a useful skill. When waiting tables, you will have to carry food from the kitchen and serve it at the table. Having the ability to remember customer orders and guest names is also really beneficial, as food orders have to be taken correctly and delivered to the right place. Guests are usually pleased if you remember their names and any regular orders. This is a nice touch, which can lead to repeat business.

Presentation skills

Presentation skills are useful if you are working within management in the future. You are likely to have to present information to other people, such as your area manager. You may have to present your ideas for a new promotion or a refurbishment, or even your financial forecasts for the coming year. Although it is not an essential part of your course, you may be asked to present information to your fellow learners or other guests so that you can practise making presentations. This will give you the opportunity to develop the skills needed to present information confidently.

Now make a list of what you think are your strongest skills at present.

Your BTEC course will help you develop all-round skills, like communication.

More about BTEC Level 2 Firsts

What is different about a BTEC Level 2 First?

How you learn

Expect to be 'hands-on'. BTEC Level 2 Firsts are practical and focus on the skills and knowledge needed in the workplace. You will learn new things and learn how to apply your knowledge.

BTEC First learners are expected to take responsibility for their own learning and be keen and well-organised. You should enjoy having more freedom, while knowing you can still ask for help or support if you need it.

How you are assessed

Many BTEC First courses are completed in one year, but if you are taking GCSEs as well, you may be doing it over two years or more. You will be assessed by completing **assignments** written by your tutors. These are based on **learning outcomes** set by Edexcel. Each assignment will have a deadline.

Case study: What's different about a BTEC?

Gary is 16. The hospitality industry really interests him. He considers that one of his strengths is being able to meet and feel at ease with people of all backgrounds.

'There are a variety of ways to get into the hospitality industry. I had the choice to do GCSEs and then go to college, or take the BTEC Level 2 First in Hospitality at school. I chose to do a BTEC because there are no exams. My friends always did far better than me in exams, as I learn better by doing things, rather than looking at theory and writing it down. Studying this BTEC has made me realise my capabilities. It's just that we all learn in different ways. I'm really good at learning from experiences rather than from a book. That's why I'm doing well with my BTEC. If you want to do

well, you have to work hard. But you get out of it what you put in. I want to go to catering college, so need to get good results.

'I've really improved since I started this course. The first few things I made needed improving, but I soon learned with practice. The tutor talked things through with me and explained what had happened. He could often tell just by looking, like the time I used plain instead of self-raising flour and my cake didn't rise. He showed me how I needed to do things differently to get them right. He didn't mind us making mistakes because he said we'd learn from them. And we all did. It wasn't long before I was pretty good at cooking and serving food. Doing the BTEC made me realise my abilities.'

Getting the most from your BTEC

Getting the most from your BTEC involves several skills, such as using your time effectively and working well with other people. Knowing yourself is also important.

Knowing yourself

How would you describe yourself? Make some notes here.

If you described yourself to someone else, would you be able to sum up your temperament and personality, identify your strengths and weaknesses and list your skills? If not, is it because you've never thought about it or because you honestly don't have a clue?

Learning about yourself is often called self-analysis. You may have already done personality tests or careers profiles. If not, there are many available online. However, the information you gain from these profiles is useless unless you can apply it to what you are doing.

Your personality

Everyone is different. For example, some people:
- like to plan in advance; others prefer to be spontaneous
- love being part of a group; others prefer one or two close friends
- enjoy being the life and soul of the party; others prefer to sit quietly and feel uncomfortable at large social gatherings
- are imaginative and creative; others prefer to deal only with facts
- think carefully about all their options before making a decision; others follow their 'gut instincts' and often let their heart rule their head.

Case study: Adam finds a course that works for him

Adam left school at 16. He took this course at college because he really wants to go into the hospitality industry.

'I soon found myself in a realistic hospitality environment to learn in when I started the course. I knew there would be a lot to do when I took this option. A really good thing about it is that there are no exams as it's all coursework. This took some of the stress away from me because I could do the work in my own time.

'The practical work, especially the front office work and front of house, is really good and I am doing really well, but I have been concerned that my coursework wouldn't be as strong. My tutor has reassured me. He has given me feedback on early drafts, which has helped me get to grips with areas I need to work on to improve my grade. He tells me the likely grade a piece of work would achieve, which means I have the opportunity to work harder to get the best grade that I can.

'At the beginning of the course I thought I'd do the minimum work needed to get a pass, but my tutor's comments have encouraged me to do more. Before I knew it, his suggestions for improvements led me to get better grades. This style works well for me because the improvement is gradual and I don't feel out of my depth. It also allows my tutor to know the stage I am at, so he explains things I am unsure about at a level I can understand. I like the way that this course gives me the opportunity to have one-to-one feedback on both the practical activities and my written work.'

TRY THIS

Imagine one of your friends is describing your best features. What would they say?

Personalities in the workplace

There's a mix of personalities in most workplaces. Some people prefer to work behind the scenes, such as many IT practitioners, who like to concentrate on tasks they enjoy doing. Others love high-profile jobs where they may often be involved in high-pressure situations, such as paramedics and television presenters. Most people fall somewhere between these two extremes.

In any job there will be some aspects that are more appealing and interesting than others. If you have a part-time job you will already know this. The same thing applies to any course you take!

Your personality and your BTEC First course

Understanding your personality means you can identify which parts of your course you are likely to find easy and which more difficult. Working out the aspects you need to develop should be positive. You can also think about how your strengths and weaknesses may affect other people.

- Natural planners find it easier to schedule work for assignments.
- Extroverts like giving presentations and working with others but may overwhelm quieter team members.
- Introverts often prefer to work alone and may be excellent at researching information.

Activity: What is your personality type?

1a) Identify your own personality type, either by referring to a personality test you have done recently or by going online and doing a reliable test. Go to page 90 to find out how to access an online test.

Print a summary of the completed test or write a brief description of the results for future reference.

b) Use this information to identify the tasks and personal characteristics that you find easy or difficult.

> **BTEC FACT**
>
> All BTEC First courses enable you to develop your personal, learning and thinking skills (**PLTS**), which will help you to meet new challenges more easily. (See page 81.)

	Easy	Difficult
Being punctual		
Planning how to do a job		
Working neatly and accurately		
Being well organised		
Having good ideas		
Taking on new challenges		
Being observant		
Working with details		
Being patient		
Coping with criticism		
Dealing with customers		
Making decisions		
Keeping calm under stress		
Using your own initiative		

	Easy	Difficult
Researching facts carefully and accurately		
Solving problems		
Meeting deadlines		
Finding and correcting own errors		
Clearing up after yourself		
Helping other people		
Working as a member of a team		
Being sensitive to the needs of others		
Respecting other people's opinions		
Being tactful and discreet		
Being even-tempered		

2 Which thing from your 'difficult' list do you think you should work on improving first? Start by identifying the benefits you will gain. Then decide how to achieve your goal.

Your knowledge and skills

You already have a great deal of knowledge, as well as practical and personal skills gained at school, at home and at work (if you have a part-time job). Now you need to assess these to identify your strengths and weaknesses.

To do this accurately, try to identify evidence for your knowledge and skills. Obvious examples are:

- previous qualifications
- school reports
- occasions when you have demonstrated particular skills, such as communicating with customers or colleagues in a part-time job.

TOP TIPS

The more you understand your own personality, the easier it is to build on your strengths and compensate for your weaknesses.

Part-time jobs give you knowledge and skills in a real work setting.

Activity: Check your skills

1 Score yourself from 1 to 5 for each of the skills in the table below.

1 = I'm very good at this skill.

2 = I'm good but could improve this skill.

3 = This skill is only average and I know that I need to improve it.

4 = I'm weak at this skill and must work hard to improve it.

5 = I've never had the chance to develop this skill.

Enter the score in the column headed 'Score A' and add today's date.

2 Look back at the units and topics you will be studying for your course – you entered them into the chart on page 9. Use this to identify any additional skills that you know are important for your course and add them to the table. Then score yourself for these skills, too.

3 Identify the main skills you will need in order to be successful in your chosen career, and highlight them in the table.

Go back and score yourself against each skill after three, six and nine months. That way you can monitor your progress and check where you need to take action to develop the most important skills you will need.

English and communication skills	Score A	Score B (after three months)	Score C (after six months)	Score D (after nine months)
Test dates:				
Reading and understanding different types of texts and information				
Speaking to other people face to face				
Speaking clearly on the telephone				
Listening carefully				
Writing clearly and concisely				
Presenting information in a logical order				
Summarising information				
Using correct punctuation and spelling				
Joining in a group discussion				
Expressing your own ideas and opinions appropriately				
Persuading other people to do something				
Making an oral presentation and presenting ideas clearly				

ICT skills	Score A	Score B (after three months)	Score C (after six months)	Score D (after nine months)
Test dates:				
Using ICT equipment correctly and safely				
Using a range of software				
Accurate keyboarding				
Proofreading				
Using the internet to find and select appropriate information				
Using ICT equipment to communicate and exchange information				
Producing professional documents which include tables and graphics				
Creating and interpreting spreadsheets				
Using PowerPoint				

Maths and numeracy skills	Score A	Score B (after three months)	Score C (after six months)	Score D (after nine months)
Test dates:				
Carrying out calculations (eg money, time, measurements etc) in a work-related situation				
Estimating amounts				
Understanding and interpreting data in tables, graphs, diagrams and charts				
Comparing prices and identifying best value for money				
Solving routine and non-routine work-related numerical problems				

Case study: John's knowledge and skills base

John started his BTEC last year when he was 14. He chose to take the hospitality course as he thought it really suited him. He got some advice from the careers adviser at school, who spoke to him about his knowledge and skills, and the areas of strength that he could develop. When John had thought about his existing knowledge and skills, he realised with help from the advisor that hospitality would be a suitable course. John had good knowledge of food and food products from studying food technology. His practical cooking skills had also been recognised as good by his food technology teacher and he really enjoyed cooking. His hygiene practices were very good and he was already aware of health and safety requirements for kitchens and food service.

Since starting his BTEC, John's tutor has been impressed by his interpersonal and presentation skills. In addition, John has good organisation skills and can work to deadlines. Being organised and able to work to deadlines are very important skills, especially for BTEC as the assignments are set with deadlines and the work needs to be organised to ensure the relevant criteria are met.

Being creative is also an important part of John's skills base. He has to prepare menus during his course, so showing creativity with both the graphical presentation of the menu and with the food ideas to go on the menu itself are important. He also has some good ICT skills. which come in useful when he designs a menu.

On reflection, after his first year of BTEC hospitality, John is really glad he has taken the course. His prior knowledge and skills with food and his interpersonal skills have proved to be really useful.

Managing your time

Some people are brilliant at managing their time. They do everything they need to and have time left over for activities they enjoy. Other people complain that they don't know where the time goes.

Which are you? If you need help to manage your time – and most people do – you will find help here.

Why time management is important

- It means you stay in control, get less stressed and don't skip important tasks.
- Some weeks will be peaceful, others will be hectic.
- The amount of homework and assignments you have to do will vary.
- As deadlines approach, time always seems to go faster.
- Some work will need to be done quickly, maybe for the next lesson; other tasks may need to be done over several days or weeks. This needs careful planning.
- You may have several assignments or tasks to complete in a short space of time.
- You want to have a social life.

Avoiding time-wasting

We can all plan to do work, and then find our plans go wrong. There may be several reasons for this. How many of the following do *you* do?

Top time-wasting activities
1 Allowing (or encouraging) people to interrupt you.
2 Not having the information, handouts or textbook you need because you've lost them or lent them to someone else.
3 Chatting to people, making calls or sending texts when you should be working.
4 Getting distracted because you simply must keep checking out MySpace, Facebook or emails.
5 Putting off jobs until they are a total nightmare, then panicking.
6 Daydreaming.
7 Making a mess of something so you have to start all over again.

Planning and getting organised

The first step in managing your time is to plan ahead and be well organised. Some people are naturally good at this. They think ahead, write down their commitments in a diary or planner, and store their notes and handouts neatly and carefully so they can find them quickly.

How good are your working habits?

Talking to friends can take up a lot of time.

Improving your planning and organisational skills

1 Use a diary or planner to schedule working times into your weekdays and weekends.

2 Have a place for everything and everything in its place.

3 Be strict with yourself when you start work. If you aren't really in the mood, set a shorter time limit and give yourself a reward when the time is up.

4 Keep a diary in which you write down exactly what work you have to do.

5 Divide up long or complex tasks into manageable chunks and put each 'chunk' in your diary with a deadline of its own.

6 Write a 'to do' list if you have several different tasks. Tick them off as you go.

7 Always allow more time than you think you need for a task.

TRY THIS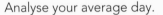

Analyse your average day.

How many hours do you spend sleeping, eating, travelling, attending school or college, working and taking part in leisure activities?

How much time is left for homework and assignments?

Case study: Managing your time

Claire is in her second year of a BTEC Level 2 First in Hospitality.

'In my first year I wasn't sure how much hard work would be expected of me, or whether the course would be lots of fun but not much work. The tutor soon made it clear what was expected of us, so the majority of my class concentrated on getting the most out of the course. I also made some good friends that I could rely on to help me if I needed it, so we soon became a team who worked together and helped each other out.

'Although it feels flexible, there is a lot of structure to the course due to routines associated with hospitality. This was really good for me as familiarising myself with them through practice taught me

to be organised. This prepared me for the work placement I'd chosen to do. Preparing, cooking and serving food to staff at school took the stress and worry out of going to my placement because I gained a lot of experience through doing it. Making mistakes and learning from them in the classroom saved me from a lot of embarrassment in the work place. The experience I gained made me useful in the restaurant kitchen.

'I could have spent my first year using my time badly and not really concentrating on my course but I'm glad I didn't. Trying really hard and focusing on what I needed to learn has led to me being offered a job at my work placement when I leave school.'

Activity: Managing time

1 The correct term for something you do in preference to starting a particular task is a 'displacement activity'. In the workplace this includes things like often going to the water cooler to get a drink, and constantly checking emails and so on online. People who work from home may tidy up, watch television or even cook a meal to put off starting a job.

Write down *your* top three displacement activities.

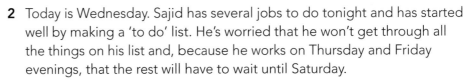

2 Today is Wednesday. Sajid has several jobs to do tonight and has started well by making a 'to do' list. He's worried that he won't get through all the things on his list and, because he works on Thursday and Friday evenings, that the rest will have to wait until Saturday.

a) Look through Sajid's list and decide which jobs are top priority and *must* be done tonight and which can be left until Saturday if he runs out of time.

b) Sajid is finding that his job is starting to interfere with his ability to do his assignments. What solutions can you suggest to help him?

Jobs to do

– File handouts from today's classes

– Phone Tom (left early today) to tell him the time of our presentation tomorrow has been changed to 11 am

– Research information online for next Tuesday's lesson

– Complete table from rough notes in class today

– Rewrite section of leaflet to talk about at tutorial tomorrow

– Write out class's ideas for the charity of the year, ready for course representatives meeting tomorrow lunchtime

– Redo handout Tom and I are giving out at presentation

– Plan how best to schedule assignment received today – deadline 3 weeks

– Download booklet from website ready for next Monday's class

Getting the most from work experience

On some BTEC First courses, all learners have to do a **work placement**. On others, like the BTEC Level 2 First in Hospitality, they are recommended but not essential. If you are doing one, you need to prepare so that you get the most out of it. The checklists in this section will help.

Before you go checklist

1. Find out about the organisation by researching online.

2. Check that you have all the information you'll need about the placement.

3. Check the route you will need to take and how long it will take you. Always allow longer on the first day.

4. Check with your tutor what clothes are suitable and make sure you look the part.

5. Check that you know any rules or guidelines you must follow.

6. Check that you know what to do if you have a serious problem during the placement, such as being too ill to go to work.

7. Talk to your tutor if you have any special personal concerns.

8. Read the unit(s) that relate to your placement carefully. Highlight points you need to remember or refer to regularly.

9. Read the assessment criteria that relate to the unit(s) and use these to make a list of the information and evidence you'll need to obtain.

10. Your tutor will give you an official logbook or diary – or just use a notebook. Make notes each evening while things are fresh in your mind, and keep them safely.

While you're on work placement

Ideally, on your first day you'll be told about the business and what you'll be expected to do. You may even be allocated to one particular member of staff who will be your 'mentor'. However, not all firms operate like this, and if everyone is very busy, your **induction** may be rushed. If so, stay positive and watch other people to see what they're doing. Then offer to help where you can.

> ### BTEC FACT
> If you need specific evidence from a work placement for a particular unit, your tutor may give you a logbook or work diary, and will tell you how you will be assessed in relation to the work that you will do.

> ### TRY THIS
> You're on work experience. The placement is interesting and related to the job you want to do. However, you've been watching people most of the time and want to get more involved. Identify three jobs you think you could offer to do.

While you're there

1. Arrive with a positive attitude, knowing that you are going to do your best and get the most out of your time there.

2. Although you may be nervous at first, don't let that stop you from smiling at people, saying 'hello' and telling them your name.

3. Arrive punctually – or even early – every day. If you're delayed for any reason, phone and explain. Then get there as soon as you can.

4. If you take your mobile phone, switch it off when you arrive.

5. If you have nothing to do, offer to help someone who is busy or ask if you can watch someone who is doing a job that interests you.

6. Always remember to thank people who give you information, show you something or agree that you can observe them.

7. If you're asked to do something and don't understand what to do, ask for it to be repeated. If it's complicated, write it down.

8. If a task is difficult, start it and then check back that you are doing it correctly before you go any further.

9. Obey all company rules, such as regulations and procedures relating to health and safety and using machinery, the use of IT equipment, and access to confidential information.

10. Don't rush off as fast as you can at the end of the day. Check first with your mentor or supervisor whether you can leave.

TOP TIPS

Observing people who are skilled at what they do helps you learn a lot, and may even be part of your **assignment brief.**

Coping with problems

Problems are rare but can happen. The most common ones are being bored because you're not given any work to do or upset because you feel someone is treating you unfairly. Normally, the best first step is to talk to your mentor at work or your supervisor. However, if you're very worried or upset, you may prefer to get in touch with your tutor instead – do it promptly.

Getting experience of work in the hospitality industry

Work experience is a very valuable opportunity for all learners. If you are applying to work at a local establishment in order to gain experience in the hospitality industry, it is important to present yourself well and to ensure you represent your school or college appropriately.

a) Write a list of important factors to consider before applying for work experience. For example, is it the right type of establishment for you?

1

2

3

b) Write down important information you need to know from an employer before you start. For example, where is the employer's business based?

1

2

3

c) Write down three things that will create a good first impression when meeting an employer, such as introducing yourself confidently.

1

2

3

d) Jake has applied to work at a hotel for his work experience, and has been accepted to work in the front office. This is something Jake has not done before, as most of his experience has been in the kitchen. He has to think about the important things he needs to know and do before and during his placement.

   i) Think of things that Jake should know about before starting his placement. Draw a spider diagram in the space overleaf.

ii) Write down three things Jake might be asked to do at his work experience in the front office.

1

2

3

iii) Write down three important skills you would need to work in the front office.

1

2

3

e) Fiona chooses to work in a restaurant for her work experience, and the manager said that she could work in the kitchen. She will be working alongside the other chefs as a comis chef, helping and supporting the smooth running of the kitchen. Imagine you are Fiona and about to start work in the kitchen. She wants to be prepared and wants to think about the things she will be asked to do.

i) Write a list of tasks that a comis chef would do when working in an industrial kitchen.

1

2

3

ii) Think about three health and safety issues that relate to working in an industrial kitchen as a chef.

1

2

3

iii) Make a list of three skills Fiona needs to be a comis chef in an industrial kitchen.

1

2

3

Case study: Kate makes the most of work experience

Kate is working at Coolings wine bar for a term on work experience. She works once a week at the wine bar. It attracts a mixed clientele, serving really good fresh food. There are opportunities to work in the kitchen or front of house taking orders and serving food.

She started at the wine bar after her first year of a BTEC Level 2 First in Hospitality. By then, Kate was confident about working front of house, taking orders, serving guests and taking payments. She therefore decided that working front of house would be best for her at the wine bar, as she was good at it. She gained more confidence and more experience dealing with the guests and became very comfortable with her role and responsibilities.

After the half term Kate thought it would be good to continue working front of house. On the first day back she spoke to the general manager who was impressed with her work but suggested that as she was so confident and competent front of house that she may learn different skills if she works in the kitchen.

Kate was nervous when she first started in the kitchen, but the kitchen staff are really nice and friendly. She now works on her own section producing garnishes and salads in the morning. At lunch service she works on the pass, plating food and calling the waiters to collect and serve. Working on the pass gave her greater understanding of not only what's required to work in the kitchen but also of food service and the link between kitchen and front of house.

The experience she is gaining in the kitchen is really beneficial. She is much more confident in the kitchen and has a better understanding of the operation. She realises that in order to make the most of work experience you need to really make an effort and take all the opportunities that are available. In that way, you learn more.

Working with other people

Everyone finds it easy to work with people they like and far harder with those they don't. On your course you'll often be expected to work as a team to do a task. This gives you practice in working with different people.

You will be expected to:
- contribute to the task
- listen to other people's views
- adapt to other people's ways of working
- take responsibility for your own contribution
- agree the best way to resolve any problems.

These are quite complex skills. It helps if you understand the benefits to be gained by working cooperatively with other people and know the best way to achieve this.

BTEC FACT

An important part of your BTEC course is learning how to work positively and productively with other people.

Case study: Jamal learns lesson in team work

Jamal is 16. He is at college taking a BTEC First in Hospitality. He copes well with working under pressure on his college courses. He makes sure that coursework is handed in on time, and he completes all tasks and assignments within the set deadlines.

Jamal and his fellow learners are going to run the kitchen and the front of house service for some special events they are planning as part of their course. This brings a different type of pressure and they have to learn to cope.

Weeks before the events are scheduled, they plan the style and type of event, from the guest numbers to the food that will be served and the level service that will be provided. Everyone has a chance to suggest ideas and to decide on what will happen. The others within Jamal's group have very different ideas about what they should do. Jamal realises that being able to compromise and resolve issues within the group is very important.

Communication is one of the most important skills needed by every member of the group. People need to communicate their ideas clearly, and let others know what they want and what they could do to help. Jamal's group knows that it will be very important for the learners serving to communicate well with the learners in the kitchen producing the food, and vice versa.

Jamal understands that you get the best outcome when you work in a team and everybody pulls in the same direction. The guests will get served on time with well prepared food and beverages. You can't do this job on your own – it needs a team effort.

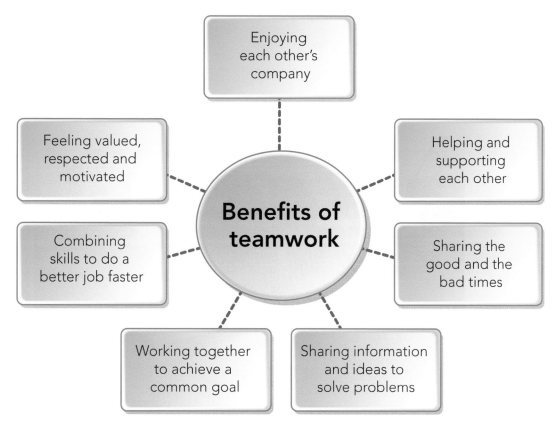

The benefits of good working relationships and teamwork

Activity: Working with other people

Millie is a learner who is currently on work experience at a large five star hotel that has over 100 employees. She has to work closely with the kitchen brigade but often works alongside other members of staff.

a) Why is it important that Millie should be able to communicate and work with all the members of staff? Write down three ideas:

1

2

3

b) Why is it important to have leadership in a group? Write down three ideas:

1

2

3

c) What qualities would you look for in a fellow colleague in the hospitality industry?

1

2

3

There are many benefits to be gained from working as a team.

Golden rules for everyone (including the team leader!)

The secret of a successful team is that everyone works together. The role of the team leader is to make this as easy as possible by listening to people's views and coordinating everyone's efforts. A team leader is not there to give orders.

Positive teamwork checklist

✔ Be loyal to your team, including the team leader.

✔ Be reliable and dependable at all times.

✔ Be polite. Remember to say 'please' and 'thank you'.

✔ Think before you speak.

✔ Treat everyone the same.

✔ Make allowances for individual personalities. Give people 'space' if they need it, but be ready to offer support if they ask for it.

✔ Admit mistakes and apologise if you've done something wrong – learn from it but don't dwell on it.

✔ Give praise when it's due, give help when you can, and thank people who help you.

✔ Keep confidences, and any promises that you make.

Do you:

a) shrug and say nothing in case he gets upset

b) ask why he didn't text you to give you warning

c) say that it's the last time you'll ever go anywhere with him and walk off?

Which do you think would be the most effective – and why?

In the planning stages of a project, it is often how things are said that will cause problems within a group. Keeping calm and not being personal with comments will ensure that issues can be dealt with in a constructive manner.

Look at the comments in the table below and see if you can rephrase what has been said to make it sound more constructive.

What was said	How could this have been said?
Why should we always do what you want?	
You're only doing the planning because I don't want to	
We all think that's a stupid idea	
I can afford it; money is no issue to me	

Getting the most from special events

BTEC First courses usually include several practical activities and special events. These enable you to find out information, develop your skills and knowledge in new situations, and enjoy new experiences. They may include visits to external venues, visits from specialist speakers, and team events.

Most learners enjoy the chance to do something different. You'll probably look forward to some events more than others. If you're ready to get actively involved, you'll usually gain the most benefit. It also helps to make a few preparations!

Case study: Yvonne prepares for a visit to a hotel

Yvonne is 15 and studying at school. Her group is going to visit a hotel and she really wants to get the most out of the trip.

She is usually well organised, but she wants to make sure that she doesn't miss out on any important information from the visit. Her tutor advises that she should think of a way of recording information during the trip. There will also be a chance to ask questions about the hotel and how it works.

Before the day of visit Yvonne thinks that the best thing to do is to conduct some initial research. She decides to find out some facts about the hotel she needs but wouldn't

necessarily have to time to get during the visit. This will allow her to spend her time getting other information straight from the people who work in the hotel.

She uses the hotel's website to find out basic facts about its facilities, service, food and beverage menus, and size. She records these facts on a factsheet.

She then prepares some questions to ask when she arrives. These are questions that she could not answer in her research or they are questions such as 'do you enjoy working in the kitchen' which have subjective answers.

Special events checklist

✔ Check you understand how the event relates to your course.

✔ If a visit or trip is not something you would normally find very interesting, try to keep an open mind. You might get a surprise!

✔ Find out what you're expected to do, and any rules or guidelines you must follow, including about your clothes or appearance.

✔ Always allow enough time to arrive five minutes early, and make sure you're never late.

✔ On an external visit, make notes on what you see and hear. This is essential if you have to write about it afterwards, use your information to answer questions in an assignment or do something practical.

✔ If an external speaker is going to talk to your class, prepare a list of questions in advance. Nominate someone to thank the speaker afterwards. If you want to record the talk, it's polite to ask first.

✔ For a team event, you may be involved in planning and helping to allocate different team roles. You'll be expected to participate positively in any discussions, to talk for some (but not all) of the time, and perhaps to volunteer for some jobs yourself.

✔ Write up any notes you make as soon as you can – while you can still understand what you wrote!

 **TRY THIS**

At the last minute, you're asked to propose a vote of thanks to a visiting speaker on behalf of your class. What would you say?

Activity: Hotel visit

Andrew Green is the general manager of a five star hotel. He has invited a group of hospitality learners from his former school to visit. They will be able to look around the hotel and meet various members of staff. At the end of the tour, Andrew will conduct a question and answer session about the various job roles within the hotel.

Imagine that you are one of the learners who will be attending the question and answer session.

a) Write down three questions that will help you find out the main roles and responsibilities of a job within a hotel that interests you:

1

2

3

b) Write down a further three questions to find out about the main skills and qualities needed to be successful in this job:

1

2

3

c) Write three questions to find out information about career progression within the hotel or about Andrew Green's career within hospitality:

1

2

3

What are the benefits of finding out this information direct from Andrew Green rather than from research using the internet?

Resources and research

Understanding resources

Resources are items that help you do something. The most obvious one is money! To obtain your BTEC First award, however, your resources are rather different.

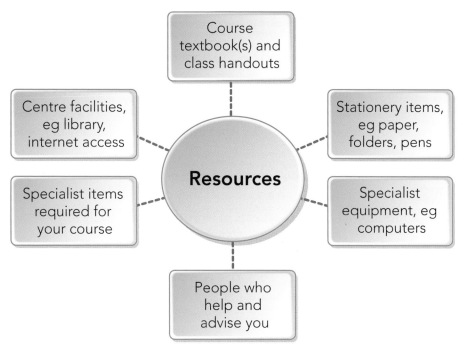

Different kinds of resources

Physical resources

Physical resources are things like textbooks, computers and any specialist equipment.

- Popular textbooks, laptops for home use and specialist equipment may need to be booked. Leaving it until the last minute is risky.

- You can ask for help if you don't know how to use resources properly.

- You should check what stationery and equipment you need at the start of your course and make sure you have it.

- You need to look after your resources carefully. This saves money and time spent replacing lost items.

People as resources

There are many people who can help you through your course:

- family members who help and support you
- your tutor
- friends in your group who collect handouts for you and phone you to keep you up to date when you're absent
- librarians and computer technicians at your centre or your local library
- expert practitioners.

Expert practitioners

Expert practitioners have worked hard to be successful in their chosen area. They have the skills and knowledge needed to do the job properly. They can be invaluable when you're researching information (see page 47). You can also learn a lot by watching them at work, especially if you can ask them questions about what they do, what they find hard, and any difficulties they've had.

Try to observe more than one expert practitioner:

- It gives you a better picture about what they do.
- No single job will cover all aspects of work that might apply to your studies.
- You may find some experts more approachable and easy to understand than others. For example, if someone is impatient because they're busy it may be difficult to ask them questions, or if someone works very quickly you may find it hard to follow what they're doing.

If you have problems, just note what you've learned and compare it with your other observations. And there's always the chance that you're observing someone who's not very good at their job! You'll only know this for certain if you've seen what people should be doing.

Activity: Create your own resource list

Suppose your course tutor has conducted a lesson on preparing for running a hospitality event. The tutor explains that you now need to put what have learned into practice. You will be in charge of organising an event from start to finish. This event will be a finger buffet for staff at your school or college. You will have the use of a school kitchen and the hall. There are many different elements that you will need prepare and organise.

a) Produce a spider diagram in the space opposite to identify some of the resources that you will need in order to promote the event.

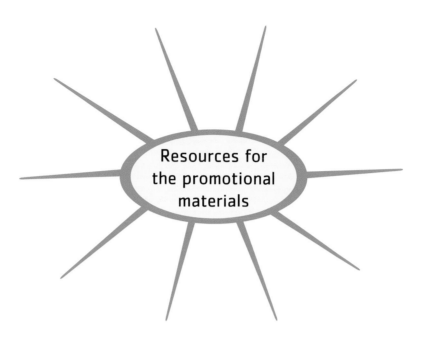

b) Write down three kitchen resources that would be needed for preparation of the finger buffet.

1

2

3

c) Write down three resources that would be needed to prepare the hall for use as the eating area.

1

2

3

Finding the information you need

The information explosion

There are lots of different ways to find out information – books, newspapers, magazines, television, radio, CDs, DVDs, the internet. And you can exchange information with other people by texting, sending an email or phoning someone.

All this makes it much easier to obtain information. If you know what you're doing, you can probably find most of what you need sitting at a computer. But there are some dangers:

- Finding exactly what you want online takes skill. You need to know what you're doing.
- It's easy to get too much information and become overwhelmed.
- It's unlikely that everything you need will be available online.
- The information you read may be out of date.
- The information may be neither reliable nor true.

> **Define what you are trying to find.** (The more precise you are, the more likely you are to find what you're looking for.)
>
> **Know where to look for it.** (Remember: the internet is not the only source of information.)
>
> **Recognise when you have found appropriate information.**
>
> **Know what to do with information once you've found it.** (Make sure that you understand it, interpret it correctly and record the source where you found it.)
>
> **Know when to stop looking** (especially if you have a deadline).

Finding and using information effectively

Finding information about the hospitality industry

Getting information about the various aspects of hospitality has become easier as more information becomes available on the internet. However, using libraries and interviewing people working in hospitality directly are also very valuable ways of collecting information.

There are many other places where you can ask questions and gather information. The tourist information board can often give some very useful information about hospitality establishments in the area, including details on facilities, products and services. It will also have information on local attractions, places of interest and upcoming events. Sometimes you can obtain local area maps that highlight hospitality establishments.

Suppliers to the hospitality industry can also be very helpful, as they can provide price lists for commodities and equipment catalogues. Suppliers may also have information on the safe transportation and checking of products and on hygiene-related issues.

You get an insight into what people expect from a hospitality establishment by questioning the general public and fellow learners or by asking them to complete questionnaires. You should get honest responses from most people if the questions are well written.

Before you start

There are four things that will help you look in the right place and target your search properly.

Ask yourself …	Because …	Example
Exactly what do I need to find out?	It will save you time and effort.	If you need information about accidents, you need to know what type of accident and over what time period.
Why do I need this information and who is going to read it?	This puts the task into context. You need to identify the best type of information to obtain and how to get it.	If you're making a poster or leaflet for children, you'll need simple information that can be presented in a graphical format. If, however, you're giving a workplace presentation on accidents, you'll need tables and graphs to illustrate your talk.
Where can I find it?	You need to consider whether your source is trustworthy and up to date. The internet is great, but you must check that the sites you use are reliable.	To find out about accidents in the workplace you could talk to the health and safety at work officer. To find examples of accidents in your local area you could look through back copies of your local newspaper in the local library or newspaper offices.
What is my deadline?	You know how long you have to find the information and use it.	

TRY THIS

Schedule your research time by calculating backwards from the deadline date. Split the time you have 50/50 between searching for information and using it. This stops you searching for too long and getting lots of interesting material, but then not having the time to use it properly!

Your three main sources of information are:

- libraries or learning resource centres
- the internet
- asking other people, for example through interviews and questionnaires.

Researching in libraries

You can use the learning resource centre in your school or college, or a local public library. Public libraries usually have a large reference section with many resources available for loan, including CD-ROMs, encyclopaedias, government statistics, magazines, journals and newspapers, and databases such as Infotrac, which contains articles from newspapers and magazines over the last five years.

The librarian will show you how to find the resources you need and how to look up a specific book (or author) to check if it is available or is out on loan.

Some books and resources can only be used in the library itself, while others can be taken out on short-term or long-term loan. You need to plan how to access and use the resources that are popular or restricted.

Using your library

✔ If your centre has an intranet you might be able to check which books and CD-ROMs are available without actually visiting the library.

✔ All libraries have photocopying facilities, so take enough change with you to copy articles that you can't remove. Write down the source of any article you photocopy, ie the name and the date of the publication.

✔ Learn how to keep a reference file (or bibliography) in which you store the details of all your sources and references. A bibliography must include CDs, DVDs and other information formats, not just books and magazines.

✔ If your search is complicated, go at a quiet time when the librarian can help you.

✔ Don't get carried away if you find several books that contain the information you need. Too many can be confusing.

✔ Use the index to find information quickly by searching for key words. Scan the index using several likely alternatives.

✔ Only use books that you find easy to understand. A book is only helpful if you can retell the information in your own words.

Researching online

A good search engine such as Google will help you find useful websites. They look for sites based on the information you enter in the search box. In some cases, such as Ask.co.uk, you may get the chance to refine your choice after entering your key words or question.

TRY THIS

Search engines don't just find websites. On Google, the options at the top of your screen include 'images', 'news' and 'maps'. If you click on 'more' and then 'even more', you'll find other options, too. You'll usually find the most relevant information if you use the UK version of a search engine. Only search the whole web if you deliberately want to include European and American information. Go to page 90 to find out how you can see this in action.

Finding information on a website

Wikipedia is a popular free online encyclopaedia. It has been criticised because entries may be inaccurate as members of the public can edit the site. However, Wikipedia is trying to prevent this by organising professional editing.

If you're not sure whether something you read is correct, or if there is anything strange about it, check it against information on another site. Make sure you ask your tutor's opinion, too.

With large websites, it can be difficult to find what you need. Always read the whole screen – there may be several menus in different parts of the screen.

To help you search, many large websites have:

- their own search facility or a site map that lists site content with links to the different pages
- links to similar sites where you might find more information. Clicking a link should open a new window, so you'll still be connected to the original site.

There are several other useful sites you could visit when researching online.

- **Directory sites** show websites in specific categories so you can focus your search at the start.
- **Forums** are sites, or areas of a website, where people post comments on an issue. They can be useful if you want to find out opinions on a topic. You can usually read them without registering.
- **News sites** include the BBC website as well as the sites for all the daily newspapers. Check the website of your local newspaper, too.

TRY THIS

Go to page 90 to find out how to access a website where you can see how directory sites work.

TOP TIPS

Bookmark sites you use regularly by adding the URL to your browser. How to do this will depend on which browser (such as Internet Explore and Firefox) you use.

There may be useful information and links at the top, foot or either side of a web page.

Printing information

- Only print information that you're sure will be useful. It's easy to print too much and find yourself drowning in paper.
- Make quick notes on your print-outs so that you remember why you wanted them. It will jog your memory when you're sorting through them later.
- If there's a printer-friendly option, use it. It will give you a print-out without unnecessary graphics or adverts.
- Check the bottom line of your print-outs. It should show the URL for that page of the website, and the date. You need those if you have to list your sources or if you want to quote from the page.

Researching by asking other people

You're likely to do this for two reasons:

- you need help from someone who knows a lot about a topic
- you need to find out several people's opinions on something.

Information from an expert

Explain politely why you are carrying out the investigation. Ask questions slowly and clearly about what they do and how they do it. If they don't mind, you could take written notes so you remember what they tell you. Put the name and title of the person, and the date, at the top. This is especially important if you might be seeing more than one person, to avoid getting your notes muddled up.

Ask whether you may contact them again, in case there's anything you need to check. Write down their phone number or email address. Above all, remember to say 'thank you'!

Case study: Tim's approach to research

Tim has found that one of the best ways to conduct research into the hospitality industry and get good answers and information is by asking people direct questions. Tim has almost completed his BTEC First in Hospitality. He has gained essential knowledge and skills on his course, acquiring both knowledge and new skills. All the units he has taken have required some element of research to get information that would help him complete the assignments in some way.

'Usually I have carried out research by using the internet and the library and by asking people questions. Using the internet is very convenient as you can use search engines to find information. This is easy, especially when it is a straightforward question and simple answer. It is the same with the library, it just takes a bit longer to find the information you need.

'Asking people is a really good way of getting information, especially if they are working in hospitality. It sometimes takes a while to arrange an interview, but it is always worth it. If the person doesn't know the answer to a question, they can often suggest someone else to ask. You get first-hand information and you can also get people's opinion on things.'

The opinions of several people

The easiest way to do this is with a questionnaire. You can either give people the questionnaire to complete themselves, or interview them and complete it yourself. Professional interviewers often telephone people to ask questions, but at this stage it's not a good idea unless you know the people you're phoning and they're happy for you to do this.

Devising a questionnaire

1   Make sure it has a title and clear instructions.

2   Rather than ask for opinions, give people options, eg yes/no, maybe/always, never/sometimes. This will make it easier to analyse the results.

3   Or you can ask interviewees to give a score, say out of 5, making it clear what each number represents, eg 5 = excellent, 3 = very good.

4   Keep your questionnaire short so that your interviewees don't lose interest. Between 10 and 15 questions is probably about right, as long as that's enough to find out all you need.

5   Remember to add 'thank you' at the end.

6   Decide upon the representative sample of people you will approach. These are the people whose views are the most relevant to the topic you're investigating.

7   Decide how many responses you need to get a valid answer. This means that the answer is representative of the wider population. For example, if you want views on food in your canteen, it's pointless only asking five people. You might pick the only five people who detest (or love) the food it serves.

TOP TIPS

Design your questionnaire so that you get quantifiable answers. This means you can easily add them up to get your final result.

TRY THIS

Always test your draft questionnaire on several people, to highlight any confusing questions or instructions.

Activity: Research

Intercontinental Hotels Group are one of the largest hotel groups in the world. Your tutor has asked you to find out more about this company. Go on the internet, find the website of Intercontinental Hotels Group and find out about:

a)   the size of Intercontinental Hotel Group

b) Six countries it covers

1

2

3

4

5

6

c) Three hotel brands that are part of the group.

1

2

3

d) Think of five questions to ask other learners in your centre to find out how much they know about the Group, and whether they know that that hotel brands you have identified are part of the Group.

1

2

3

4

5

e) Interview ten learners and summarise your results in the space below.

Managing your information

Whether you've found lots of information or only a little, assessing what you have and using it wisely is very important. This section will help you avoid the main pitfalls.

Organising and selecting your information

Organising your information

The first step is to organise your information so that it's easy to use.

- Make sure your written notes are neat and have a clear heading – it's often useful to date them, too.
- Note useful pages in any books or magazines you have borrowed.
- Highlight relevant parts of any handouts or leaflets.
- Work out the results of any questionnaires you've used.

Case study: Brad learns how to organise his work

Brad is just starting his BTEC Level 2 First in Hospitality. He knows that he will have to be well organised to complete his coursework. He decides that best thing to do is to talk to his course tutor about improving his organisation skills.

His tutor first talks to Brad about organising printed information. She suggests filing material in a lever arch file with subsections for the different course units. This would mean that Brad could find information more easily when he needed it. The same applies to computer work. Brad should create one folder for hospitality work, with subfolders for the various units. Brad could then store any relevant information in the corresponding subfolder. Organising his work like this would give Brad a good system to store his work and make it easy to retrieve information.

His tutor also suggests Brad talks to some other learners who may be able to show him the ways they organise their work.

Selecting your information

Re-read the **assignment brief** or instructions you were given, to remind yourself of the exact wording of the question(s) and divide your information into three groups:

1 Information that is totally relevant.

2 Information that is not as good, but could come in useful.

3 Information that doesn't match the questions or assignment brief very much but that you kept because you couldn't find anything better!

Check there are no obvious gaps in your information against the questions or assignment brief. If there are, make a note of them so that you know exactly what you still have to find. Although it's ideal to have everything you need before you start work, don't delay if you're short of time.

Putting your information in order

Putting your information in a logical order means you can find what you want easily. It will save you time in the long run. This is doubly important if you have lots of information and will be doing the work over several sessions.

Activity: Organising your information

Following a visit to a tourist information centre to gather information about local hotels, you have obtained a large collection of promotional leaflets. The leaflets give information on each hotel's location, prices and facilities.

Write down three ways in which you could organise or categorise the information you have collected.

1

2

3

Invitations have been sent to 20 people for an organised function. The events coordinator has requested that you keep a log or record of the replies that are received accepting or declining the invitation.

Use the space opposite space to design a log to record replies.

Interpreting and presenting your information

The next stage is to use your information to prepare the document and/or oral presentation you have to give. There are four steps:

1 Understand what you're reading.

2 Interpret what you're reading.

3 Know the best form in which to produce the information, bearing in mind the purpose for which it is required.

4 Create the required document so that it's in a suitable layout with correct spelling and punctuation.

Understanding what you read

As a general rule, never use information that you don't understand. However, nobody understands complex or unfamiliar material the first time they read it, especially if they just scan through it quickly. Before you reject it, try this:

Read it once to get the main idea.	Read it again, slowly, to try to take in more detail.	Look up any words you don't know in a dictionary to find out what they mean.
Write your own version.	Summarise the main points in your own words.	Read it a third time and underline or highlight the main points. (If this is a book or magazine that you shouldn't write in, take a photocopy first and write on that.)

Special note: Show both the article and your own version to your tutor to check your understanding. This will help you identify any points you missed out and help you improve your skills of interpreting and summarising.

Understanding unfamiliar information

Interpreting what you read

Interpreting what you read is different from understanding it. This is because you can't always take it for granted that something you read means what it says. The writer may have had a very strong or biased opinion, or may have exaggerated for effect. This doesn't mean that you can't use the information.

Strong opinions and bias

People often have strong points of view about certain topics. This may be based on reliable facts, but not always! We can all jump to conclusions that may not be very logical, especially if we feel strongly about something.

Things aren't always what they seem to be. Are these boys fighting or are they having a good time?

Exaggeration

Many newspapers exaggerate facts to startle and attract their readers.

LOCAL FIRM DOUBLES STAFF IN TWO WEEKS!

This newspaper headline sounds very positive. You could easily think it means employment is growing and there are more jobs in your area. Then you read on, and find the firm had only four staff and now has eight!

Tables and graphs

You need to be able to interpret what the figures mean, especially when you look at differences between columns or rows. For example, your friend might have an impressive spreadsheet that lists his income and expenditure. In reality, it doesn't tell you much until you add the figures up and subtract one from the other. Only then can you say whether he is getting into debt. And even if he is, you need to see his budget over a few months, rather than just one which may be exceptional.

Choosing a format

You may have been given specific instructions about the format and layout of a document you have to produce, in which case life is easy as long as you follow them! If not, think carefully about the best way to set out your information so that it is clear.

TRY THIS

There are many scare stories in the media about issues such as immigration, children's reading ability or obesity. Next time you're watching television and these are discussed, see if you can spot biased views, exaggeration and claims without any supporting evidence.

TOP TIPS

Never make assumptions or jump to conclusions. Make sure you have all the evidence to support your views.

Different formats	Example
text	when you write in paragraphs or prepare a report or summary
graphical	a diagram, graph or chart
pictorial	a drawing, photograph, cartoon or pictogram
tabular	numerical information in a table

The best method(s) will depend on the information you have, the source(s) of your material and the purpose of the document – a leaflet for schoolchildren needs graphics and pictures to make it lively, whereas a report to company shareholders would be mainly in text form with just one or two graphs.

Stating your sources

Whatever format you use, if you are including other people's views, comments or opinions, or copying a table or diagram from another publication, you must state the source by including the name of the author, publication or the web address. This can be in the text or as part of a list at the end. Failure to do this (so you are really pretending other people's work is your own) is known as **plagiarism**. It is a serious offence with penalties to match.

Text format

Creating written documents gets easier with practice. These points should help.

TOP TIPS

Don't just rely on your spellchecker. It won't find a word spelled wrongly that makes another valid word (eg from/form), so you must proofread everything. And remember to check whether it is set to check American English or British English. There are some spelling differences.

Golden rules for written documents

1. Think about who will be reading it, then write in an appropriate language and style.

2. Ensure it is technically correct, ie no wrong spellings or bad punctuation.

3. Take time to make it look good, with clear headings, consistent spacing and plenty of white space.

4. Write in paragraphs, each with a different theme. Leave a line space between each one.

5. If you have a lot of separate points to mention, use bullets or numbered points. Numbered points show a certain order or quantity (step 1, step 2, etc). Use bullet points when there is no suggested order.

6. Only use words that you understand the meaning of, or it might look as if you don't know what you mean.

7. Structure your document so that it has a beginning, middle and end.

8. Prepare a draft and ask your tutor to confirm you are on the right track and are using your information in the best way.

Graphical format

Most people find graphics better than a long description for creating a quick picture in the viewer's mind. There are several types of graphical format, and you can easily produce any of these if you have good ICT skills.

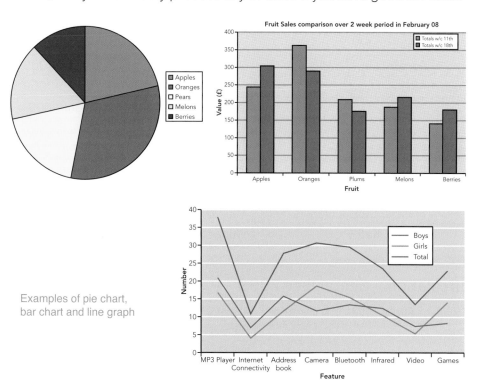

Examples of pie chart, bar chart and line graph

Pictorial format

Newspapers and magazines use pictures to illustrate situations and reduce the amount of words needed. It doesn't always have to be photographs though. For example, a new building may be sketched to show what it will look like.

A pictogram or pictograph is another type of pictorial format, such as charts which use the image of an object (fruit, coins, even pizzas) to represent data, such as the number eaten or amount spent.

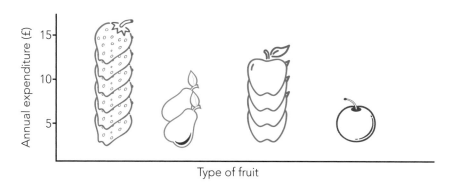

Tabular format

A table can be an easy way to communicate information. Imagine a retailer preparing information about the items in stock. Text would be difficult to understand, and comparisons between stock levels and sales would be almost impossible to make. A table, however, would easily show the fastest-selling items.

Tables are also ideal if you are showing rankings – such as best-selling music or books.

Bestsellers list – September 2009

Position	Title	Author	Imprint	Publication
1 (New)	Lost Symbol, The	Brown, Dan	Bantam Press	15-Sep-2009
2 (1)	Complaints, The	Rankin, Ian	Orion	03-Sep-2009
3 (New)	Return Journey, The	Binchy, Maeve	Orion	17-Sep-2009
4 (7)	Sapphire	Price, Katie	Century	30-Jul-2009
5 (9)	Wolf Hall	Mantel, Hilary	Fourth Estate	30-Apr-2009
6 (3)	Week in December, A	Faulks, Sebastian	Hutchinson	03-Sep-2009
7 (2	Alex Cross's Trial	Patterson, James	Century	10-Sep-2009
8 (4)	White Queen, The	Gregory, Philippa	Simon & Schuster Ltd	18-Aug-2009
9 (5)	Even Money	Francis, Dick & Francis, Felix	Michael Joseph	03-Sep-2009
10 (8)	206 Bones	Reichs, Kathy	William Heinemann	27-Aug-2009

National newspaper circulation – September 2009

	August 2009	August 2008	% change on last year	August 09 (without bulks)	March 2009 – August 2009	% change on last year
Sun	3,128,501	3,148,792	-0.64	3,128,501	3,052,480	-2.25
Daily Mail	2,171,686	2,258,843	-3.86	2,044,079	2,178,462	-4.45
Daily Mirror	1,324,883	1,455,270	-8.96	1,324,883	1,331,108	9.44
Daily Star	886,814	751,494	18.01	886,814	855,511	16.65
The Daily Telegraph	814,087	860,298	-5.37	722,644	807,328	-6.73
Daily Express	730,234	748,664	-2.46	730,234	727,824	-1.32
Times	576,185	612,779	-5.97	529,746	588,471	-4.63
Financial Times	395,845	417,570	-5.2	365,269	411,098	-6.7
Daily Record	347,302	390,197	-10.99	345,277	350,306	-10.59
Guardian	311,387	332,587	-6.37	311,387	332,790	-4.11
Independent	187,837	230,033	-18.34	148,551	198,445	-16.76

Activity: Interpreting and presenting your information

You have been asked to carry out some research on local hotels. You want information about the size of hotels in your area. You decide that a good way of judging the size of hotels is to find out the number of rooms they have for guests. After conducting some research and organising the information, you have prepared a table that sets out the number of single and double rooms that are available at each hotel which you investigated.

Hotel	Single rooms	Double rooms
White Hart	12	24
Northgate Hotel	16	42
The New Inn	4	12
The Imperial	10	46
Mount Hotel	6	28
Globe Hotel	8	32

a) Identify an appropriate method of presenting this information graphically and draw the graph below in the space provided.

You decide to continue this research into the hotels in your area by now finding out about some of the additional facilities that each offers. You focus on four facilities and find out if they are offered at each of the hotels. The tables below shows the results of this investigation.

Hotel	Swimming pool	Sauna	Multi gym	Beauty treatments
White Hart	yes	yes	yes	no
Northgate Hotel	yes	yes	yes	yes
The New Inn	yes	no	no	yes
The Imperial	yes	no	no	yes
Mount Hotel	no	no	yes	yes
Globe Hotel	no	yes	no	yes

b) Identify an appropriate method of presenting this information graphically and draw the graph below in the space provided.

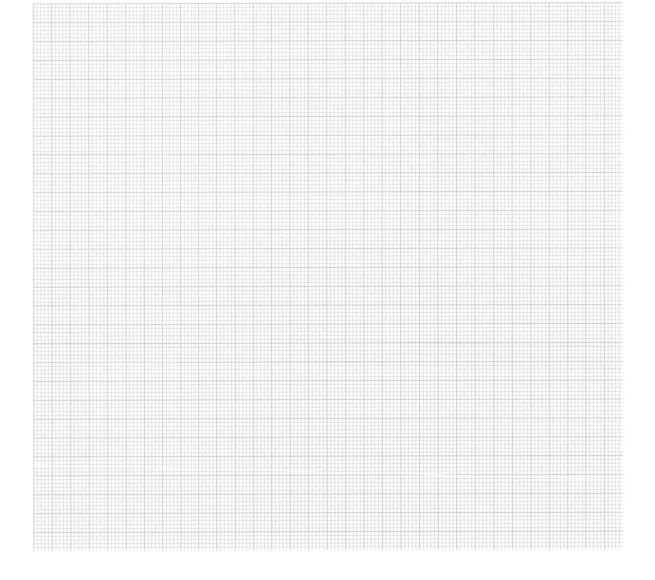

The White Hart has a rather limited menu. The general manager is thinking of changing the menu. The chef has been asked to provide some information about the current menu. In order to show the manager which dishes are the best sellers, the head chef wishes to present a chart. The chart must clearly show the relative popularity of each dish.

	Dishes sold in last 12 months
Poached salmon	1348
Rump steak	2412
Vegetarian lasagne	1198
Warm salad of chicken	843
Tuna steak	1978
Steak and kidney pudding	2262

c) Identify an appropriate method of presenting this information graphically and draw a chart in the space provided below.

Making presentations

Presentations help you to learn communication skills.

Some people hate the idea of standing up to speak in front of an audience. This is quite normal, and you can use the extra energy from nerves to improve your performance.

Presentations aren't some form of torture devised by your tutor! They are included in your course because they help you learn many skills, such as speaking in public and preparing visual aids. They also help you practise working as a team member, and give you a practical reason for researching information. And it can be far more enjoyable to talk about what you've found out rather than write about it!

There's a knack to preparing and giving a presentation so that you use your energies well, don't waste time, don't fall out with everyone around you and keep your stress levels as low as possible. Think about the task in three stages: preparation, organisation and delivery.

Preparation

Start your initial preparations as soon as you can. Putting them off will only cause problems later. Discuss the task in your team so that everyone is clear about what has to be done and how long you have to do it in.

Divide any research fairly among the team, allowing for people's strengths and weaknesses. You'll also need to agree:

- which visual aids would be best
- which handouts you need and who should prepare them
- where and when the presentation will be held, and what you should wear
- what questions you might be asked, both individually and as a team, and how you should prepare for them.

Once you've decided all this, carry out the tasks you've been allocated to the best of your ability and by the deadline agreed.

TOP TIPS

Keep visual aids simple but effective, and check any handouts carefully before you make lots of copies.

Organisation

This is about the planning you need to do as a team so that everything will run smoothly on the day.

Delivery

This refers to your performance during the presentation. Being well prepared and well organised helps you keep calm. If you're very nervous at the start, don't panic – just take a few deep breaths and concentrate on the task, not yourself. It's quite normal to be nervous at the start but this usually fades once you get under way. You might even enjoy it…

Case study: Sarah learns to conquer her nerves

Sarah always used to be nervous when it came to presenting to the rest of the group. Throughout her BTEC First in Hospitality, Sarah has delivered presentations to her own group and sometimes to hotel managers, chefs and other guests invited into college.

It has got easier with experience to stand up in front of people and talk. However, the first few times she made presentations had not been such a good experience. She had not really organised herself, prepared good resources or practised.

She has learned that she has to plan presentations well and this has made her feel more confident. When she had prepared a presentation on job roles in hospitality she practised the presentation all the way through. For the first few practices, she read out loud from prompt cards on which had key words in large writing to give her direction. When she got more confident, she practised in front of some of her fellow learners to get some constructive feedback. The other learners then practised their own presentations. During the course, they had to do practical cookery demonstrations and they would practise these together after they had cooked or completed the demonstration task a few times on their own. Sarah also timed her presentations to make sure they are always within the time limit.

Practising gives her more confidence, but making sure she is always prepared is also really important. Having everything she needs ready, such as her notes, prompt cards and other resources also makes things much easier. She makes sure that the computer and projector are working correctly well before her presentation.

TOP TIPS

Never read from prepared prompt cards! Look at the audience when you're talking and smile occasionally. If you need to use prompt cards as a reminder of what to say, write clearly so that you need only glance at them.

TOP TIPS

Remember, the audience always makes allowances for some nerves!

Activity: Making a presentation

Prepare a short presentation about the BTEC First in Hospitality for a group of learners who are considering joining the programme next year.

Use the PowerPoint slides below to present important information and make some brief notes to support your slides.

Your assessments

The importance of assignments

All learners on BTEC First courses are assessed by means of **assignments**. Each one is designed to link to specific **learning outcomes** and **grading criteria**. At the end of the course, your assignment grades put together determine your overall grade.

To get the best grade you can, you need to know the golden rules that apply to all assignments, then how to interpret the specific instructions.

10 golden rules for assignments

1 Check that you understand the instructions.

2 Check whether you have to do all the work on your own, or if you will do some as a member of a group. If you work as a team, you need to identify which parts are your own contributions.

3 Always write down any verbal instructions you are given.

4 Check the final deadline and any penalties for not meeting it.

5 Make sure you know what to do if you have a serious personal problem, eg illness, and need an official extension.

6 Copying someone else's work (**plagiarism**) is a serious offence and is easy for experienced tutors to spot. It's never worth the risk.

7 Schedule enough time for finding out the information and doing initial planning.

8 Allow plenty of time between talking to your tutor about your plans, preparations and drafts, and the final deadline.

9 Don't panic if the assignment seems long or complicated. Break it down into small, manageable chunks.

10 If you suddenly get stuck, ask your tutor to talk things through with you.

Case study: Louise gets advice on how to tackle her assignments and plan her work

Louise wants to know how the assessment process works. The tutor explains how learners will be assessed and what they have to do to meet the relevant grading criteria.

Louise makes sure that she knows the deadlines and dates to submit her coursework. It is important that she has these dates correctly entered in her diary so that her work is on time. Louise can then think about how to organise her work in the time allowed.

On receiving her first assignments, Louise is told to read each task carefully and to study the related assessment criteria. She reads the assessment criteria a few times to make sure that she addresses the right aspects in her work.

The class is told that if anyone doesn't understand a task, they should talk to their tutor, who will explain it further. They have to achieve all the pass criteria in a unit to get a pass grade for that unit and to be able to work for merit and distinction grades.

Louise looks at the first part of the assessment and grading criteria of Unit 2: Products, Services and Support in the Hospitality Industry. The pass criteria ask her to identify products and services available to customers for different hospitality businesses in the locality, the merit criteria ask her to explain which products and services are available in the hospitality industry and the distinction criteria ask her to analyse the differences between the products and services offered in different hospitality businesses.

If she needs to improve her work to get a better grade, she will need to act on feedback provided by her tutor.

Interpreting the instructions

Most assignments start with a **command word** – describe, explain, evaluate etc. These words relate to how complex the answer should be.

Command words

Learners often don't do their best because they read the command words but don't understand exactly what they have to do. These tables show you what is required for each grade when you see a particular command word.

Command words and obtaining a pass

Complete ...	Complete a form, diagram or drawing.
Demonstrate ...	Show that you can do a particular activity.
Describe ...	Give a clear, straightforward description that includes all the main points.
Identify ...	Give all the basic facts relating to a certain topic.
List ...	Write a list of the main items (not sentences).
Name ...	State the proper terms related to a drawing or diagram.
Outline ...	Give all the main points, but without going into too much detail.
State ...	Point out or list the main features.

Examples:
- **List** the main features on your mobile phone.
- **Describe** the best way to greet a customer.
- **Outline** the procedures you follow to keep your computer system secure.

Command words and obtaining a merit

Analyse ...	Identify the factors that apply, and state how these are linked and how each of them relates to the topic.
Comment on ...	Give your own opinions or views.
Compare ... Contrast ...	Identify the main factors relating to two or more items and point out the similarities and differences.
Competently use ...	Take full account of information and feedback you have obtained to review or improve an activity.
Demonstrate ...	Prove you can carry out a more complex activity.
Describe ...	Give a full description, including details of all the relevant features.
Explain ...	Give logical reasons to support your views.
Justify ...	Give reasons for the points you are making so that the reader knows what you're thinking.
Suggest ...	Give your own ideas or thoughts.

Examples:
- **Explain** why mobile phones are so popular.
- **Describe** the needs of four different types of customers.
- **Suggest** the type of procedures your employer would need to introduce to keep the IT system secure.

Command words and obtaining a distinction

Analyse ...	Identify several relevant factors, show how they are linked, and explain the importance of each.
Compare ... Contrast ...	Identify the main factors in two or more situations, then explain the similarities and differences, and in some cases say which is best and why.
Demonstrate ...	Prove that you can carry out a complex activity, taking into account information you have obtained or received to adapt your original idea.
Describe ...	Give a comprehensive description which tells a story to the reader and shows that you can apply your knowledge and information correctly.
Evaluate ...	Bring together all your information and make a judgement on the importance or success of something.
Explain ...	Provide full details and reasons to support the arguments you are making.
Justify ...	Give full reasons or evidence to support your opinion.
Recommend ...	Weigh up all the evidence to come to a conclusion, with reasons, about what would be best.

Examples:
- **Evaluate** the features and performance of your mobile phone.
- **Analyse** the role of customer service in contributing to an organisation's success.
- **Justify** the main features on the website of a large, successful organisation of your choice.

> **TRY THIS**
>
> Check the command word you are likely to see for each of your units in the **grading grid** in advance. This tells you the **grading criteria** for the unit so that you know the evidence you will have to present.

> **TOP TIPS**
>
> Think of assignments as an opportunity to demonstrate what you've learned and to get useful feedback on your work.

Activity: Planning work on an assignment task

To ensure that you complete all assignment work and meet the relevant criteria grading, it is very important to read each task carefully. Jack is studying Unit 1: Investigating the Catering and Hospitality Industry. He has been given this task.

1 You must compare and contrast the features of establishments in hospitality and catering by explaining the different features of the different sectors. The following types of hospitality business must be addressed: one hotel and whether it is budget or has a brand attached to it and the star rating if any, one restaurant, one pub, bar or nightclub, one contract food service provider, one hospitality service, one membership club and one events business. The descriptions for each business within the hospitality industry should include its location, size and whether it is local or national. Evidence could take the form of a report and should use examples from the hospitality industry at national level. **(P1)**

Suppose you have been given this task. Produce a spider diagram in the space below which sets out the things you have to do to meet the criteria and note some ideas you may have to meet the criteria.

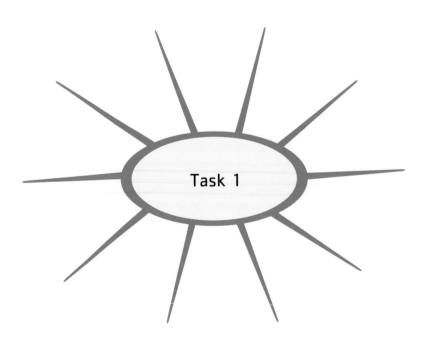

Activity: Improving your work

Lydia has been given an activity to complete. She needs to think of ways to improve her work and to ensure that she meets all the assessment criteria.

Write a list of ways she can identify where she is missing the assessment criteria and how she can improve her work. Two example answers have been provided.

Meeting assessment criteria	Improving her grade
Make sure she has checked her work against the assessment criteria grid	Act on feedback from her course tutor.

Activity: Acting on feedback

It is important to act on the feedback your course tutor provides on your assignments. You should identify any areas for improvement.

Make a list of sources of useful information or people who might be helpful in order to improve your work.

Sample assignment

Note about assignments
All learners are different and will approach their assignment in different ways.
The sample assignment that follows shows how one learner answered a brief to achieve pass,
merit and distinction level criteria. The learner work shows just one way in which grading criteria
can be evidenced. There are no standard or set answers. If you produce the required evidence
for each task then you will achieve the grading criteria covered by the assignment.

Front sheet

Complete the front sheet fully, making sure the information is correct and neatly written.

Check the completion or hand-in date and make a diary note to ensure you complete and hand in your work on time.

Check that you have provided the evidence required, which is listed in these boxes.

Learner name		Assessor name	
Karen Johnson		Anne Teacher	

Date issued	Completion date	Submitted on
10 January 2011	5 February 2011	5 February 2011

Qualification	Unit
BTEC Level 2 First Diploma In Hospitality	Unit 3 Principles of Customer Service in Hospitality, Leisure, Travel and Tourism

Assignment title	Assignment 2 – How effective is customer service?

In this assessment you will have opportunities to provide evidence against the following criteria.
Indicate the page numbers where the evidence can be found.

Criteria reference	To achieve the criteria the evidence must show that the learner is able to:	Task no.	Evidence
P6	Identify the benefits of excellent customer service for the individual	1a	Presentation, notes and observation record
P7	Describe the importance of positive attitude, behaviour and motivation in providing excellent customer service	1b	"
P8	Describe the importance of personal presentation within the industries	1c	"
P9	Explain the importance of using appropriate types of communication	1d	"
P10	Describe the importance of effective listening skills	1e	"
M2	Analyse the customer service provision in hospitality organisations	2	5
D1	Evaluate the effectiveness of the customer service provision in different hospitality organisations	3	6–7

Learner declaration
I certify that the work submitted for this assignment is my own and research sources are fully acknowledged.

Learner signature: *Karen Johnson*　　　　　　　　Date: *5 February 2011*

Make sure you have fully met each of the criteria listed here.

Sign and date the declaration, making sure the work submitted is your own and not copied or taken from other sources unless it is referenced correctly.

Assignment brief

The given scenario makes the assignment more relevant and realistic and could help you when faced with a similar situation in a future career in hospitality.

Keep a focus on the title and the purpose of the assignment. This will help to ensure that your work is relevant.

Unit title	Unit 3 Principles of Customer Service in Hospitality, Leisure, Travel and Tourism
Qualification	BTEC Level 2 First Diploma in Hospitality
Start date	10 January 2011
Deadline date	5 February 2011
Assessor	Anne Teacher

Assignment title	How effective is customer service?

The purpose of this assignment is to:
Understand the role of the individual in delivering customer service in the hospitality, leisure, travel and tourism industries.

Scenario
You are working as a customer service coach for a chain of motorway services restaurants. Your manager has asked you to give a presentation to new staff on the role of the individual in delivering customer service. You will need to use your own experiences of visiting restaurants, fast food outlets, pubs, hotels, and any other place you have experienced customer service in a hospitality organisation.

Your manager has asked you to present your findings as a PowerPoint presentation. You have also been asked to analyse and evaluate your chain, comparing it to another organisation – for this you will need to prepare a set of notes.

Task 1
This task will be assessed through your presentation and your sets of notes. Your assessor will also complete an observation record for inclusion as evidence for this task. You will be making visits to at least two hospitality organisations to observe their customer service provision.

Prepare a presentation for new staff, together with a set of notes which you will use when you give your presentation.

In your presentation:

a) Identify the benefits for the individual who is delivering excellent customer service. Consider how it can motivate staff and increase their job satisfaction, for example through working as a team or feeling loyalty to the organisation.

This provides evidence for P6

b) Describe the importance of having a positive attitude in providing excellent customer service. Consider the effect an individual's attitude, behaviour and what motivates them can have on the way they deliver customer service.

This provides evidence for P7

c) Describe the importance of personal presentation in customer service. You should explain how first impressions can count, importance of personal hygiene, and the importance of your appearance. You will need to describe types of uniform, dress codes, and regulations regarding hair, makeup and jewellery.

This provides evidence for P8

d) How you communicate with customers is also very important, not only what you say, but also your body language. Explain the importance of body language, for example posture, expression, gestures, and eye contact. You should also note the way you use your voice, for example tone, pitch, pace and appropriate language avoiding slang and jargon. You will be able to demonstrate appropriate use of body language and voice in your presentation.

This provides evidence for P9

e) Speaking is important, but so is listening and you will need to describe why listening is important when delivering customer service. For example, asking appropriate questions, repeating back to customers and looking attentive. You will be able to demonstrate these in your presentation.

This provides evidence for P10

Your presentation should last about 10 minutes. Remember that Tasks 1d and 1e could be demonstrated.

This will usually take the form of presenting your findings to the rest of your group or discussing your ideas.

Your assessor will complete an observation record to confirm that you have completed the task satisfactorily.

These sources of information can be very useful, but ensure that you explore other options in your research, such as talking to or interviewing people who work in hospitality management.

Task 2

To achieve M2 you need to analyse the customer service provision in two different hospitality organisations. For example: Why does it differ between a five star hotel and fast food outlet? What are the reasons for delivering a different customer service provision in two different organisations?

Remember to take your findings from Task 1 into account: benefits to the individual, positive attitude, difference in expected personal presentation and differences in expected communication skills. It might help if you can use two organisations with which you have had experience of being a customer or member of the staff.

Present your analysis as a set of notes.

This provides evidence for M2

Task 3

To achieve D1 you need to evaluate the effectiveness of customer service in two different organisations. To do this you will need to do a comparison of the two organisations you used for the Task 2. It is useful to visit these two places and say how effective they were in providing a customer service provision in line with the expectations of their customers.

For example, explain where they were good at meeting a high standard of customer service provision. Were there any instances where they failed to meet the expectations in their customer service provision? What could be done to improve this?

Show your findings in the form of a written report.

This provides evidence for D1

Sources of information

Your notes from your visits to hospitality organisations

Textbooks
Ovenden F, Holmes S, Horne S and Wilson P – *BTEC First Hospitality* (Heinemann Educational, 2008)
ISBN 9780435465285

Journal
Caterer and Hotelkeeper – Reed Business Publications

Websites
www.bbc.co.uk/learningzone BBC Learning Zone – programme times
www.bha.org.uk British Hospitality Association
www.caterersearch.com Caterersearch – Hospitality news
www.catersource.com Catersource – Education, products and news for caterers
www.people1st.co.uk People 1st – Sector Skills Council for Hospitality, Leisure, Travel and Tourism

This brief has been verified as being fit for purpose.			
Assessor	Anne Teacher		
Signature	Anne Teacher	Date	29 September 2010
Internal verifier	Terry Frier		
Signature	Terry Frier	Date	29 September 2010

Sample learner work

Having a title slide is very important to state your topic and give clarity to the audience.

Each slide has a title or focus and key comments that the learner can then expand on during the presentation.

Sample learner work: page 1

Slide 1

How effective is customer service?

Slide 2

Benefits of good service

- Helps motivate staff
- Gives you more job satisfaction
- Helps you work better with your colleagues
- Helps you feel loyalty to your employer

If you are working in an organisation which is giving its customers a good service you feel better at your work. If the service is poor, you will not feel so good about working there. If you work in a restaurant that has good service, you will work better as a team and feel good about the restaurant. Customer Service is all about team work and if the team are working well you will not want to let them down. It will give you pride in your work. If the service or food is bad, then you will not feel so good about working there and you may not feel like giving a good service. You may also be getting lots of complains which might upset you and you will feel bad.

This slide has listed the key features of having a positive attitude, which learner would expand on them during the presentation.

Visuals or images strengthen the ideas being put forward by the learner in the presentation.

Sample learner work: page 2

Slide 3

Having a positive attitude.

- A positive attitude rubs off on others and helps motivate them
- It will show customers you enjoy your work
- It gives customers a better service
- You feel better at your work

Slide 4

Appearance

- **Personal Hygiene**
  – clean hands and nails, daily shower, not strong smelling deodorant
- **Uniforms**
  – uniform neatly pressed and clean
- **Hair and make-up**
  – Hair clean and tied at the back. minimum make up
- **Jewellery**
  – only a wedding ring and ear studs

It helps to have a helpful attitude and try and be helpful to the customer. If they ask for something you can't provide, then say sorry and explain why. You must hide your feelings if you are grumpy and not feeling good, this will show and the customer might think this is the usual service. In some fast food outlets you can have a cheerful easy manner with customer, but in a top restaurant you need to be more formal and call the customer Sir or Madame. If you give a good service to customers, they will enjoy their meal and may well leave a good tip. This will make you feel good, especially if the customer said how much they liked your service. If you are getting tips and customers are saying how good your service was, it make you feel good and take more pride in what you are doing. The more you are praised, the harder you will work and then you get more praise (hopefully). If you give poor service they might complain and then you feel bad and this may effect how you deal with the next customer. And you could get into trouble with your boss.

No-one wants to be served by somebody looking scruffy or smells. It is important that you look clean, smart and tidy. You should use a deodorant every day but not any strong perfume or aftershave. You must keep clean, especially hands and nails. Most catering businesses supply staff with a uniform or state what you must wear. You should keep your uniform clean and pressed at all times. Make up should be limited and not too noticeable. Your hair must be clean and, if long, tied at the back. You should only wear ear studs and a wedding ring, no other jewellery.

This learner has again identified key aspects of appearance in the hospitality industry and also given examples on the slide. More details can be given during the comments made in the presentation.

A full set of means of communication is given, with examples of good and poor communication. These examples are an effective way of getting a message across to the audience.

Giving comparisons is also a good way of getting a message across. The learner would need to provide some commentary to accompany the slide.

Sample learner work: page 3

Slide 5

Communication

- Posture
- Expression
- Gestures
- Eye contact
- Voice
- Avoid slang
- Listening

Slide 6

Customer Service

A comparison between
two motorway services
food outlets

Demonstrate poor posture, slouch, and good posture upright and smiling

Demonstrate poor expression and good show eye contact and look around room whilst talking. Important to look direct at customers when you are talking to them or they are talking to you

Demonstrate poor gestures, looking up "huh", shaking head, good gestures look at them and smile, standing upright. Nodding to show you understand them.

Voice I **never** saw her. I never **saw** her. I never saw **her**. I never saw her. Smile whilst talking makes you sound more friendly, even on the phone.

Avoid slang, "cool", might be OK in MacDonald's but not in a five start hotel. "yup " in stead of yes. Some restaurants don't like "there you go" as you serve the meal.

Listening is important, show you are listening with eye contact and nodding of the head, repeat the order back. If you are not sure ask. Finish by saying "That's interesting" "I'll let chef know" this will show you were listening and understood.

The assessor will fill out and sign an observation record confirming that the task has been performed to a satisfactory standard.

The observation record will identify the criteria that are being assessed and whether they have been met.

Sample learner work: page 4

Observation record

Learner name	Karen Johnson
Qualification	BTEC Level 2 First Diploma In Hospitality
Unit number and title	Unit 3 Principles of Customer Service in Hospitality, Leisure, Travel and Tourism

Description of activity undertaken (please be as specific as possible)

Karen gave a confident presentation using a combination of PowerPoint slides and demonstration.

Notes were handed in separately, together with a print out of the presentation slides.

Assessment and grading criteria

You have achieved P6, P7, P8, P9, P10.

A very good presentation Karen, clear voice projection and confident with the Pass criteria.

You resorted to reading from your notes and this meant you lost eye contact with your audience. Try to look up more often when reading.

A very good effort to meet the grades and a very good presentation – well done Karen.

How the activity meets the requirements of the assessment and grading criteria

P6 I think you might have explained your views on motivation better, but you did mention motivation that you can get from giving good service and working as a team.

P7 You identified the importance of a positive attitude (can do) and what to do if you are unable to satisfy the customer's needs. You compared service in fast food outlets with that in restaurants. You mentioned the spiral effect saying how praise can motivate you to perform better.

P8 You covered the importance of appearance in customer service mentioning clean looks, deodorant, make up, uniform, hair and jewellery.

P9 You illustrated the importance of body language with a demonstration of poor and good posture, plus smiling and eye contact. Your demonstration on the difference that can be made by emphasising specific words in a sentence was original and showed good research. You also covered the need to avoid jargon and slang.

P10 You gave examples of good listening: eye contact, repeating orders, and suggested phrases that would indicate you had heard the customer.

Assessor name	Anne Teacher		
Assessor signature	Anne Teacher	Date	1 February 2010

The assessor will give feedback on whether and how the activity has met the assessment criteria.

Identify the task by listing the relevant task number and the criteria being addressed.

The criteria on the assignment front sheet asks the learner to analyse the customer service provision in hospitality organisations. Make sure your response meets the given criteria. You can make this clear with a heading for your task.

Sample learner work: page 5

Task 2 M2

A comparison between two motorway services food outlets

Both companies offer quick meals at motorway stations and road side service stations. Both have to provide a quick service for their customers who are travelling and only want a short stop to get something to eat. The fast food outlet also provides a drive through where you can order a meal and sit in the car and eat it. This is super quick!

The fast food outlet has bright colourful premises and employs young people to give a friendly atmosphere which appeals to children and young people. Because of the friendly atmosphere, young people enjoy working there and can take pride in working for a world-wide company. They provide a limited menu of burgers, fries, and soft drinks that are all prepared for cooking in a few minutes. Because of this the service is quick but you have to queue to be served and your meal is served on cardboard boxes and paper packets. This means turn around at the tables is very quick.

In comparison, the restaurant also provides a quick service because motorists do not want to hang around and they want to get on with their journey. You have to queue to be shown to your table. They provide a sit down service with the food brought to you by a waitresses. They also provide plates and cutlery at the table. The staff are mostly older than those at the fast food outlet, so give a more formal service. The restaurant offers a larger choice of menu but most dishes are either grilled, fried or microwaved so can be prepared quickly. They have 174 diners throughout Britain and have been going for 50 years, so staff can take pride in working for a popular and well known company.

The fast food outlet offers a smaller menu but a quicker service and their main product, the burger, is popular with young people. The restaurant offers more choice on their menu but you have to wait a short while for it to be cooked, but not as long as you might in a high-street restaurant or hotel.

Both organisations have dress codes for staff. The fast food chain choose polo shirts and baseball caps for their uniform in keeping with the young person's image, compared to the more formal dress at the restaurant.

The fast food chain has mystery shoppers who call to check that the customer service is up to the standard expected. This means that staff have to be polite to all customers in case the customer is a mystery shopper.

Both companies offer Wi-Fi at their sites for customers who need to use their laptops. Some of the fast food sites are open 24 hours, but the restaurant only opens from 7am until 8pm. This limits the number of customers because they are not open late at night

Qualified staff at the fast food place are allowed to work abroad, so when they return to Britain they will speak a foreign language and give a useful service to foreign customers. The restaurant chain is only based in Britain so doesn't offer work in other countries.

Both companies have a policy to inspect the toilets at regular times, and have a board to shown when they were last inspected.

I found the staff at the fast food place were friendly and helpful but were under pressure to serve so many customers. They used eye contact when dealing with customers, but once the order had been taken, they turn to the next customer and ignored you until your order is ready. The restaurant staff were also friendly and helpful and spent more time listening to their customer because they were not under so much pressure. They also checked with the customer if the meal was OK.

Make sure that you provide as much information as you can to meet the criteria. In this case, this means looking at all aspects of the customer service.

Task number and criteria being addressed are given. However, the title could be better and reflect what is required by the criteria.

When evaluating ensure that you have conducted enough research in order that you can reflect and evaluate correctly.

Sample learner work: page 6

Task 3 D1

Two motorway service stations food outlets

Both companies appear to meet the needs of their customer's in different ways. The fast food chain has a world-wide reputation and their customer service is well known, so they must maintain this standard. The restaurant is only known in Britain but have a long established reputation. In either company, you know what to expect because they all offer the same menu and have the same house style where ever you are.

The fast food chain have a more easy going style of customer service by making you queue to order, then a few minutes to wait for the order, whilst they serve the next customer. After the meal, you have to clear you own table and a member of the crew will then clean the table down. In busy periods they can't always do this quickly enough so customers may sit at a table that has not yet been cleaned, or may even have the previous persons rubbish still there. The restaurant has waitress service and they bring the meal to you and clear the table afterwards. As you have to wait to be shown a table, the table will always have been cleared and cleaned before you get there. The fast food place could employ more staff in busy periods to clean the tables and make sure customer's rubbish has been binned.

The fast food menu is more likely to appeal to young people and having a young staff, and wearing casual clothes as a uniform helps the image with young people and children. They also appeal to children as they give children's parties. The restaurant appeals more to older people and their uniform is more formal for this reason but they do cater for children also with a children's menu.

The fast food place offers a fast service, so staff don't always have much time to communicate with customers. They just take your order, and tell you when it is ready. Although I found they did use eye contact and good body language, the pace of their talking was very quick and may be a problem for older customers who have come in with their grandchildren for example.

The restaurant was a much slower pace and staff had time to take the order and even comment upon the weather or traffic conditions. They were also able to ask if your meal was OK, which the fast food place couldn't because they had no contact at the table with customers. Maybe The fast food place manager could come out every half hour and check customers were satisfied with their meal and service.

The service at the fast food outlet was much quicker. However, the restaurant customers could be in and out in half an hour, although some liked to linger longer over coffee reading the free newspapers provided. This would not be possible at the fast food place because the number of customers would soon block all the tables. Customers are offered a newspaper at the restaurant and the waitress will ask you if you enjoyed your meal. The fast food place does not do this because they have no contact with their customers once the meal is served

The restaurant did not seem to have all tables in use, even at Lunchtime. I think both companies appeal to different types of customer. Children probably prefer to go to a fast food place as they might find it more relaxing and they may feel they have to behave better at a restaurant. Both provide uniforms in keeping with their image and the staff are trained in customer service to meet the needs of their customers.

Fast food outlets appeal to a younger customer and offer a very quick service but it is limited to meals that younger people would choose. The restaurant offers a quick service, but not so quick as a fast food place, and offer a larger range of meals. Both are ideal for motorists as you can get a quick meal and be on your way. Both cater for their customers' needs as you may want and expect a quicker service at one or you may prefer to take more time and be served at your table at the other. The fast food place is quicker and cheaper but have a more rushed feeling where as the restaurant is dearer, but offers a more formal but relaxed feel about their restaurants.

Good use of visual images that list or identify the differences between a fast food outlet and a restaurant.

Sample learner work: page 7

To summarise their differences in customer service are:

Fast food outlet	Restaurant

Quick service	Quicker than a restaurant
Queue to be served	Table Service
Better for children	Bigger menu
Quick, friendly	Formal,
Casual Uniform	Traditional uniform
After served, left to find table	Shown to your table
Table may have left over rubbish	Table set before you get there
No check your meal is OK	Check if meal is OK

Make sure that you are meeting all the pass criteria. If you don't achieve each pass criteria, you cannot get a pass for the unit.

Give feedback about the assignment, including what you enjoyed and any problems that you came across.

Read the assessor's feedback carefully. The assessor will give valuable information on how well the criteria have been covered and if any improvements are required.

Qualification	BTEC Level 2 First Diploma In Hospitality	Assessor name	Anne Teacher
Unit number and title	Unit 3 Principles of Customer Service in Hospitality, Leisure, Travel and Tourism	Learner name	Karen Johnson

Grading criteria	Achieved?
P6 Identify the benefits of excellent customer service for the individual	Y
P7 Describe the importance of positive attitude, behaviour and motivation in providing excellent customer service	Y
P8 Describe the importance of personal presentation within the industries	Y
P9 Explain the importance of using appropriate types of communication	Y
P10 Describe the importance of effective listening skills	Y
M2 Analyse the customer service provision in hospitality organisations	Y
D1 Evaluate the effectiveness of the customer service provision in different hospitality organisations	Y

Learner feedback

I found this assignment easy as I was able to visit the fast food outlet and the restaurant

Assessor feedback

You have covered all the unit content including a good demonstration of body language and voice tone and listening skills. **P6** could have been covered in more depth, but there is sufficient to award the grade. The other criteria were covered sufficiently to award the grade. You made good use of your demonstrations for **P9** and **P10**.

See my comments on the Observation sheet

M2 Your notes made a comparison between the fast food outlet and the restaurant. You compared the atmosphere at the two outlets, and the different customer service provision. You might have clarified how "formal" the restaurant is, it is really only their uniform, as service can be friendly – did you not find this? You also compared the customer contact communication at the two outlets.

D1 You evaluated the different customer service provision and explain similarities and differences. You mentioned the difference in table service as opposed to no table service at the fast food outlet, and made a suggestion for improvement at the fast food outlet. (Note – the restaurant also has waiters!) You mentioned the difference in typical customer in the two organisations and how this is reflected in their service provision. You made suggestions for improvements on this at the fast food outlet. You identified the time taken to serve customers and identified why the fast food outlet couldn't encourage customers to stay longer. You finished with a short summary. You could have included the service at the restaurant for customers in a hurry – they do offer a coffee and sandwich take out service.

Action plan

You have achieved merit and distinction criteria, so there are no actions needed – Well done Karen

Assessor signature	Anne Teacher	Date	10 February 2011
Learner signature	Karen Johnson	Date	10 February 2011

The assessor will let you know if you have achieved the criteria.

The assessor has not provided any action plan for further work in this case as the learner has achieved all the criteria.

Coping with problems

Most learners sail through their BTEC First with no major problems. Unfortunately, not everyone is so lucky. Some may have personal difficulties or other issues that disrupt their work so they are late handing in their assignments. If this happens to you, it's vital to know what to do. This checklist should help.

Checklist for coping with problems

✔ Check that you know who to talk to.

✔ Don't sit on a problem and worry about it. Talk to someone promptly, in confidence. It's always easier to cope if you've shared it with someone.

✔ Most centres have professional counsellors you can talk to if you prefer. They won't repeat anything you say to them without your permission.

✔ If you've done something wrong or silly, people will respect you more if you are honest, admit where you went wrong and apologise promptly.

TOP TIPS

If you have a serious complaint or concern, talk to your chosen tutor first – for example if you believe an assignment grade is unfair. All centres have official procedures to cover important issues such as appeals about assignments and formal complaints, but it's usually sensible to try to resolve a problem informally first.

Case study: Don't ignore your problems

Issie knows that she should deal with any problems rather than ignore them. It is much easier to get help and to rectify or resolve any problems rather than leave them until they build up.

One problem she encountered was at her work placement. She had been there for a while but was always doing the same task – salad prep. She really wanted to do some different jobs, so she could get more experience and gain some new skills. The other chefs were happy for her to work in their sections, but it had to be cleared with the manager first.

Issie spoke to her manager to see if she could move sections and he told her to 'leave it with him',

but two weeks later nothing had happened. She decided to speak to her tutor about the problem. Her tutor was really good and discussed the situation with her and then spoke to the placement. The tutor had found out that the manager had simply forgotten about Issie's concerns and had not spoken to the head chef.

The next time Issie had a work placement day she was moved to a different section. The manager even apologised to her for not addressing the problem sooner. She also said that in future Issie was always welcome to come directly to her with any problems, which may sort things out more quickly.

Activity: Knowing where to get help

Knowing where to go if you have a problem is really important. Find out who you should meet to discuss the following problems or issues.

Issue or problem	Where would you go for help?
You don't understand why you have been given a low grade for an assignment	
You have problems at home which are affecting your work	
You are struggling with understanding your work	
You are having problems with another learner who is bullying you	
You have changed you mind about what you might want to do in your career	

Skills building

To do your best in your assignments you need a number of skills, including:

- your **personal, learning and thinking skills**
- your **functional skills** of ICT, mathematics and English
- your proofreading and document-production skills.

Personal, learning and thinking skills (PLTS)

These are the skills, personal qualities and behaviour that you find in people who are effective and confident at work. These people enjoy carrying out a wide range of tasks, always try to do their best, and work well alone or with others. They enjoy a challenge and use new experiences to learn and develop.

Activity: How good are your PLTS?

1 Do this quiz to help you identify areas for improvement.

   a) I get on well with other people.

      Always   Usually   Seldom   Never

   b) I try to find out other people's suggestions for solving problems that puzzle me.

      Always   Usually   Seldom   Never

   c) I plan carefully to make sure I meet my deadlines.

      Always   Usually   Seldom   Never

   d) If someone is being difficult, I think carefully before making a response.

      Always   Usually   Seldom   Never

   e) I don't mind sharing my possessions or my time.

      Always   Usually   Seldom   Never

   f) I take account of other people's views and opinions.

      Always   Usually   Seldom   Never

   g) I enjoy thinking of new ways of doing things.

      Always   Usually   Seldom   Never

   h) I like creating new and different things.

      Always   Usually   Seldom   Never

   i) I enjoy planning and finding ways of solving problems.

      Always   Usually   Seldom   Never

j) I enjoy getting feedback about my performance.

Always   Usually   Seldom   Never

k) I try to learn from constructive criticism so that I know what to improve.

Always   Usually   Seldom   Never

l) I enjoy new challenges.

Always   Usually   Seldom   Never

m) I am even-tempered.

Always   Usually   Seldom   Never

n) I am happy to make changes when necessary.

Always   Usually   Seldom   Never

o) I like helping other people.

Always   Usually   Seldom   Never

Score 3 points for each time you answered 'Always', 2 points for 'Usually', 1 point for 'Seldom' and 0 points for 'Never'. The higher your score, the higher your personal, learning and thinking skills.

2 How creative are you? Test yourself with this activity. Identify 50 different objects you could fit into a matchbox at the same time! As a start, three suitable items are a postage stamp, a grain of rice, a staple. Can you find 47 more?

BTEC FACTS

Your BTEC First qualification is at Level 2. Qualifications in functional skills start at Entry level and continue to Level 2. (You don't need to achieve functional skills to gain any BTEC qualification, and the evidence from a BTEC assignment can't be used towards the assessment of functional skills.)

Functional skills

Functional skills are the practical skills you need to function confidently, effectively and independently at work, when studying and in everyday life. They focus on the following areas:

- Information and Communications Technology (ICT)
- Maths
- English.

You may already be familiar with functional skills. Your BTEC First tutors will give you more information about how you will continue to develop these skills on your new course.

ICT skills

These will relate directly to how much 'hands-on' practice you have had on IT equipment. You may be an experienced IT user, and using word-processing, spreadsheet and presentation software may be second nature. Searching for information online may be something you do every day – in between downloading music, buying or selling on eBay and updating your Facebook profile!

Or you may prefer to avoid computer contact as much as possible. If so, there are two things you need to do.

1 Use every opportunity to improve your ICT skills so that you can start to live in the 21st century!

2 Make life easier by improving your basic proofreading and document preparation skills.

Proofreading and document preparation skills

Being able to produce well-displayed work quickly will make your life a lot easier. On any course there will be at least one unit that requires you to use good document preparation skills.

Tips to improve your document production skills
✔ If your keyboarding skills are poor, ask if there is a workshop you can join. Or your library or resource centre may have software you can use.
✔ Check that you know the format of documents you have to produce for assignments. It can help to have a 'model' version of each type in your folder for quick reference.
✔ Practise checking your work by reading word by word – and remember not to rely on spellcheckers.

Activity: How good are your ICT skills?

1a) Test your current ICT abilities by responding *honestly* to each of the following statements.

   i) I can create a copy of my timetable using a word-processing or spreadsheet package.
   True   False

   ii) I can devise and design a budget for myself for the next three months using a spreadsheet package.
   True   False

   iii) I can email a friend who has just got broadband to say how to minimise the danger of computer viruses, what a podcast is, and also explain the restrictions on music downloads.
   True   False

   iv) I can use presentation software to prepare a presentation containing four or five slides on a topic of my choice.
   True   False

   v) I can research online to compare the performance and prices of laptop computers and prepare an information sheet using word-processing software.
   True   False

   vi) I can prepare a poster, with graphics, for my mother's friend, who is starting her own business preparing children's party food, and attach it to an email to her for approval.
   True   False

TRY THIS

Learning to touch-type can save you hours of time. Go to page 90 to find out how to access a website where you can check your keyboarding skills.

TOP TIPS

Print your work on good paper and keep it flat so that it looks good when you hand it in.

1b) Select any one of the above to which you answered false and learn how to do it.

2 Compare the two tables below. The first is an original document; the second is a typed copy. Are they identical? Highlight any differences you find and check them with the key on page 89.

Name	Date	Time	Room
Abbott	16 July	9.30 am	214
Grey	10 August	10.15 am	160
Johnston	12 August	2.20 pm	208
Waverley	18 July	3.15 pm	180
Jackson	30 September	11.15 am	209
Gregory	31 August	4.20 pm	320
Marshall	10 September	9.30 am	170
Bradley	16 September	2.20 pm	210

Name	Date	Time	Room
Abbott	26 July	9.30 am	214
Gray	10 August	10.15 am	160
Johnson	12 August	2.20 pm	208
Waverley	18 July	3.15 am	180
Jackson	31 September	11.15 am	209
Gregory	31 August	4.20 pm	320
Marshall	10 September	9.30 pm	170
Bradley	16 August	2.20 pm	201

Maths or numeracy skills

Four easy ways to improve your numeracy skills

1 Work out simple calculations in your head, like adding up the prices of items you are buying. Then check if you are correct when you pay for them.

2 Set yourself numeracy problems based on your everyday life. For example, if you are on a journey that takes 35 minutes and you leave home at 11.10 am, what time will you arrive? If you are travelling at 40 miles an hour, how long will it take you to go 10 miles?

3 Treat yourself to a Maths Training program.

4 Check out online sites to improve your skills. Go to page 90 to find out how to access a useful BBC website.

TOP TIPS

Quickly test answers. For example, if fuel costs 85p a litre and someone is buying 15 litres, estimate this at £1 x 15 (£15) and the answer should be just below this. So if your answer came out at £140, you'd immediately know you'd done something wrong!

Activity: How good are your maths skills?

Answer as many of the following questions as you can in 15 minutes. Check your answers with the key on page 89.

1 a) 12 + 28 = ?

      i) 30   ii) 34   iii) 38   iv) 40   v) 48

  b) 49 ÷ 7 = ?

      i) 6   ii) 7   iii) 8   iv) 9   v) 10

  c) ½ + 1¼ = ?

      i) ¾   ii) 1½   iii) 1¾   iv) 2¼   v) 3

  d) 4 × 12 = 8 × ?

      i) 5   ii) 6   iii) 7   iv) 8   v) 9

  e) 16.5 + 25.25 – ? = 13.25

      i) 28.5   ii) 31.25   iii) 34.5   iv) 41.65   v) 44

2 a) You buy four items at £1.99, two at 98p and three at £1.75. You hand over a £20 note. How much change will you get? _____

  b) What fraction of one litre is 250 ml? _____

  c) What percentage of £50 is £2.50? _____

  d) A designer travelling on business can claim 38.2p a mile in expenses. How much is she owed if she travels 625 miles? _____

  e) You are flying to New York in December. New York is five hours behind British time and the flight lasts eight hours. If you leave at 11.15 am, what time will you arrive? _____

  f) For your trip to the United States you need American dollars. You find that the exchange rate is $1.5 dollars.

    i) How many dollars will you receive if you exchange £500? _____

    ii) Last year your friend visited New York when the exchange rate was $1.8. She also exchanged £500. Did she receive more dollars than you or fewer – and by how much? _____

  g) A security guard and his dog patrol the perimeter fence of a warehouse each evening. The building is 480 metres long and 300 metres wide and the fence is 80 metres out from the building on all sides. If the guard and his dog patrol the fence three times a night, how far will they walk? _____

English skills

Your English skills affect your ability to understand what you read, prepare a written document, say what you mean and understand other people. Even if you're doing a practical subject, there will always be times when you need to leave someone a note, tell them about a phone call, read or listen to instructions – or write a letter for a job application!

Six easy ways to improve your English skills

1 Read more. It increases the number of words you know and helps to make you familiar with correct spellings.

2 Look up words you don't understand in a dictionary and check their meaning. Then try to use them yourself to increase your vocabulary.

3 Do crosswords. These help increase your vocabulary and practise your spelling at the same time.

4 You can use websites to help you get to grips with English vocabulary, grammar and punctuation. Go to page 90 to find out how to access a useful BBC website.

5 Welcome opportunities to practise speaking in class, in discussion groups and during presentations – rather than avoiding them!

6 Test your ability to listen to someone else by seeing how much you can remember when they've finished speaking.

Activity: How good are your English skills?

1 In the table below are 'wrong' versions of words often spelled incorrectly. Write the correct spellings on the right. Check your list against the answers on page 89.

Incorrect spelling	Correct spelling
accomodation	
seperate	
definate	
payed	
desparate	
acceptible	
competant	
succesful	

2 Correct the error(s) in these sentences.

a) The plug on the computer is lose.

b) The car was stationery outside the house.

c) Their going on they're holidays tomorrow.

d) The principle of the college is John Smith.

e) We are all going accept Tom.

3 Punctuate these sentences correctly.

a) Toms train was late on Monday and Tuesday.

b) She is going to France Belgium Spain and Italy in the summer.

c) He comes from Leeds and says its great there.

4 Read the article on copyright.

Copyright

Anyone who uses a photocopier can break copyright law if they carry out unrestricted photocopying of certain documents. This is because The Copyright, Designs and Patents Act 1988 protects the creator of an original work against having it copied without permission.

Legally, every time anyone writes a book, composes a song, makes a film or creates any other type of artistic work, this work is treated as their property (or copyright). If anyone else wishes to make use of it, they must get permission to do so and, on occasions, pay a fee.

Licences can be obtained to allow educational establishments to photocopy limited numbers of some publications. In addition, copies of an original document can be made for certain specific purposes. These include research and private study. Under the Act, too, if an article is summarised and quoted by anyone, then the author and title of the original work must be acknowledged.

a) Test your ability to understand unfamiliar information by responding to the following statements with 'True' or 'False'.

i) Students and tutors in schools and colleges can copy anything they want.
True   False

ii) The law which covers copyright is The Copyright, Designs and Patents Act 1988.
True   False

iii) A student photocopying a document in the library must have a licence.
True   False

iv) Copyright only relates to books in the library.
True   False

v) If you quote a newspaper report in an assignment, you don't need to state the source.
True   False

vii) Anyone is allowed to photocopy a page of a book for research purposes.
True   False

b) Make a list of key points in the article, then write a brief summary in your own words.

5 Nikki has read a newspaper report that a horse racing in the Kentucky Derby had to be put down. The filly collapsed and the vet couldn't save her. Nikki says it's the third time in two years a racehorse has had to be put down in the US. As a horse lover she is convinced racing should be banned in Britain and the US. She argues that fox hunting was banned to protect foxes, and that racehorses are more important and more expensive than foxes. Darren disagrees. He says the law is not working, hardly anyone has been prosecuted and fox hunting is going on just like before. Debbie says that animals aren't important whilst there is famine in the world.

a) Do you think the three arguments are logical? See if you can spot the flaws and check your ideas with the suggestions on page 89.

b) Sporting activities and support for sporting teams often provoke strong opinions. For a sport or team of your choice, identify two opposing views that might be held. Then decide how you would give a balanced view. Test your ideas with a friend or family member.

Answers

Skills building answers

ICT activities

2 Differences between the two tables are highlighted in bold.

Name	Date	Time	Room
Abbott	**16** July	9.30 am	214
Grey	10 August	10.15 am	160
Johnston	12 August	2.20 pm	208
Waverley	18 July	3.15 **pm**	180
Jackson	**30** September	11.15 am	209
Gregory	31 August	4.20 pm	320
Marshall	10 September	9.30 **am**	170
Bradley	16 **September**	2.20 pm	**210**

Maths/numeracy activities

1 **a)** iv, **b)** ii, **c)** iii, **d)** ii, **e)** i

2 **a)** £4.83, **b)** ¼, **c)** 5%, **d)** £238.75, **e)** 2.15 pm, **f) i)** $750 **ii)** $150 dollars more, **g)** 6.6 km.

English activities

1 Spellings: accommodation, separate, definite, paid, desperate, acceptable, competent, successful

2 Errors:
a) The plug on the computer is <u>loose</u>.
b) The car was <u>stationary</u> outside the house.
c) <u>They're</u> going on <u>their</u> holidays tomorrow.
d) The <u>principal</u> of the college is John Smith.
e) We are all going <u>except</u> Tom.

3 Punctuation:
a) Tom's train was late on Monday and Tuesday.
b) She is going to France, Belgium, Spain and Italy in the summer.
c) He comes from Leeds and says it's great there.

4 **a) i)** False, **ii)** True, **iii)** False, **iv)** False, **v)** False, **vi)** False, **vii)** True

5 A logical argument would be that if racehorses are frequently injured in a particular race, eg one with difficult jumps, then it should not be held. It is not logical to compare racehorses with foxes. The value of the animal is irrelevant if you are assessing cruelty. Darren's argument is entirely different and unrelated to Nikki's. Whether or not fox hunting legislation is effective or not has no bearing on the danger (or otherwise) to racehorses. Finally, famine is a separate issue altogether. You cannot logically 'rank' problems in the world to find a top one and ignore the others until this is solved!

Accessing website links

Links to various websites are referred to throughout this BTEC Level 2 First Study Skills Guide. In order to ensure that there links are up-to-date, that they work and that the sites aren't inadvertently linked to any material that could be considered offensive, we have made links available on our website: www.pearsonhotlinks.co.uk. When you visit the site, please enter the title BTEC Level 2 First Study Skills Guide in Hospitality or the ISBN 9781846909245 to gain access to the website links and information on how they can be used to help you with your studies.

Useful terms

Apprenticeships
Schemes that enable you to work and earn money at the same time as you gain further qualifications (an NVQ award and a technical certificate) and improve your functional skills. Apprentices learn work-based skills relevant to their job role and their chosen industry. Go to page 90 to find out how to access useful websites.

Assessment methods
Methods, such as practical tasks and assignments, which are used to check that your work demonstrates the learning and understanding you need to obtain the qualification.

Assessor
The tutor who marks or assesses your work.

Assignment
A complete task or mini-**project** set to meet specific grading criteria.

Assignment brief
The information and instructions related to a particular assignment.

BTEC Level 3 Nationals
Qualifications you can take when you have successfully achieved a Level 2 qualification, such as BTEC First. They are offered in a variety of subjects.

Credit value
The number of credits attached to your BTEC course. The credit value increases relative to the length of time you need to complete the course, from 15 credits for a BTEC Certificate, to 30 credits for a BTEC Extended Certificate and 60 credits for a BTEC Diploma.

Command word
The word in an assignment that tells you what you have to do to produce the type of answer that is required, eg 'list', 'describe', 'analyse'.

Educational Maintenance Award (EMA)
This is a means-tested award which provides eligible learners under 19 who are studying a full-time course at a centre with a cash sum of money every week. Go to page 90 to find out how to access useful websites.

Functional skills
The practical skills that enable all learners to use and apply English, Maths and ICT both at work and in their everyday lives. They aren't compulsory to achieve on the course, but are of great use to you.

Grade
The rating of pass, merit or distinction that is given to an assignment you have completed, which identifies the standard you have achieved.

Grading criteria
The standard you have to demonstrate to obtain a particular grade in the unit. In other words, what you have to prove you can do.

Grading grid
The table in each unit of your BTEC qualification specification that sets out the grading criteria.

Indicative reading
Recommended books, magazines, journals and websites whose content is both suitable and relevant to the unit.

Induction
A short programme of events at the start of a course or work placement designed to give you essential information and introduce you to other people so that you can settle in easily.

Internal verification
The quality checks carried out by nominated tutors at all centres to ensure that all assignments are at the right level and cover appropriate learning outcomes. The checks also ensure that all **assessors** are marking work consistently and to the same standards.

Learning outcomes

The learning and skills you must demonstrate to show that you have learned a unit effectively.

Levels of study

The depth, breadth and complexity of knowledge, understanding and skills required to achieve a qualification determines its level. Level 2 is equivalent to GCSE level (grades A* to C). Level 3 equates to GCE A-level. As you successfully achieve one level, you can progress on to the next. BTEC qualifications are offered at Entry Level, then Levels 1, 2, 3, 4, 5, 6 and 7.

Mandatory units

On a BTEC Level 2 First course, these are the compulsory units that all learners must complete to gain the qualification.

Optional units

Units on your course from which you may be able to make a choice. They help you specialise your skills, knowledge and understanding, and may help progression into work or further education.

Personal, learning and thinking skills (PLTS)

The skills and qualities that improve your ability to work independently and be more effective and confident at work. Opportunities for developing these are a feature of all BTEC First courses. They aren't compulsory to achieve on the course, but are of great use to you.

Plagiarism

Copying someone else's work or work from any other sources (eg the internet) and passing it off as your own. It is strictly forbidden on all courses.

Portfolio

A collection of work compiled by a learner – for an **assessor** – usually as evidence of learning.

Project

A comprehensive piece of work which normally involves original research and planning and investigation, either by an individual or a team. The outcome will vary depending upon the type of project undertaken. For example, it may result in the organisation of a specific event, a demonstration of a skill, a presentation, or a piece of writing.

Tutorial

An individual or small group meeting with your tutor at which you discuss the work you are currently doing and other more general course issues.

Unit content

Details about the topics covered by the unit and the knowledge and skills you need to complete it.

Work placement

Time spent on an employer's premises when you carry out work-based tasks as an employee and also learn about the enterprise to develop your skills and knowledge.

Work-related qualification

A qualification designed to help you to develop the knowledge and understanding you need for a particular area of work.